You Can't Help But Listen

To Max and Lois
In The name of The Lord
Charles R. Munson

You Can't Help But Listen

User-Friendly Oral Communication

Charles R. Munson

With Bill Butterworth

Herald
Press

Scottdale, Pennsylvania
Waterloo, Ontario

Library of Congress Cataloging-in-Publication Data
Munson, Charles R., 1919-
  You can't help but listen : user-friendly oral communication / by
Charles R. Munson ; with Bill Butterworth.
    p. cm.
  Includes bibliographical references.
  ISBN 0-8361-9132-3 (alk. paper)
  1. Public speaking.   2. Public speaking—Religious aspects—
Christianity. I. Butterworth, Bill. II. Title.
PN4121 .M76 2001
808.5'1—dc21   00-050579

YOU CAN'T HELP BUT LISTEN
Copyright © 2001 by Herald Press, Scottdale, Pa. 15683, USA
    Published simultaneously in Canada by Herald Press,
    Waterloo, Ont. N2L 6H7. All rights reserved
Library of Congress Catalog Card Number: 00-050579
International Standard Book Number: 0-8361-9132-3
Printed in the United States of America
Book design by Merrill R. Miller
Cover photo by Jiang Jin, SuperStock

10 09 08 07 06 05 04 03 02 01 10 9 8 7 6 5 4 3 2 1

To order or request information, please call
1-800-759-4447 (individuals); 1-800-245-7894 (trade).
Website: www.mph.org

In loving memory of
my wife, Aida May,
and
to my daughters,
Bonnie and Deborah

CONTENTS

FOREWORD

Who's the speaker today?" I heard these words coming from one of my buddies across the clubhouse at Jacob's Field in Cleveland. It was Sunday morning and time for our weekly chapel service.

"A guy I've never heard of," I answered. "Someone named Munson."

I had no idea what to expect.

Over the past nineteen years in major-league baseball, I had heard hundreds of chapel speakers, from fifteen to twenty minutes each. My teammates and I had listened to talks from former professional athletes, local pastors, Christian businessmen, and traveling chapel speakers.

The only thing I knew about Charles Munson that July morning in 1997 was that he had spent many years as a pastor and college professor. *Pastor* sounded fine. *College professor* made me a little nervous. As I rounded the corner to the doorway of the small room where the Indians held chapel, I got my first glimpse of Dr. Munson.

He could have been my grandfather. He was quite tall—perhaps an athlete as a young man—but the years had rounded his shoulders and whitened his hair. He walked with a cane.

I went straight to him and introduced myself. "I'm

Orel Hershiser," I said as I shook his hand.

"Charles Munson . . . no, not Charles Manson," our speaker said with a mischievous twinkle in his eye. I liked him right away.

Thirty minutes later, Charles (though he had multiple graduate degrees, he insisted I not call him Dr. Munson) concluded his talk with a short prayer. During chapel, my teammates and I had been treated to one of the most creative, attention-capturing presentations we had ever heard. This elderly gentleman, more than three times the age of most of the men who listened that morning, had held us spellbound. We had been given a strong dose of truth, cleverly layered between illustrations, humor, and stories. This was no ordinary pastor and certainly no typical college professor!

Following the talk, I walked up to Charles. "That was one of the most wonderful and helpful chapel talks I have ever heard," I said with a smile. And then I added, almost as an afterthought, "Have you ever put your ideas on creative speaking in a book?"

My humble friend was taken back. "Uh, no, I haven't," he answered, giving me the same winsome smile my teammates had seen many times that morning. I thanked him for his message and said good-bye.

I'm going to find a way to get Charles's ideas in a book, I told myself as I walked back to my locker to put on my uniform. *There are so many people who could be helped by his approach to effective communication.*

Less than two weeks later, I was with my good friend Robert D. Wolgemuth. In addition to being my business partner, Robert is a literary agent. I told him about Charles. In a few days, Robert had contacted Dr. Munson and Bill Butterworth, a gifted collaborative writer and communicator in his own right. Together, Charles and Bill wrote the book you now hold in your hand.

As one of Charles Munson's biggest fans, I commend this book to you. It comes from a lifetime of obedient living and a career dedicated to effective communication. It's filled with practical advice guaranteed to help you be a better leader, teacher, coach, minister, or parent. And it captures what I experienced the first time I heard this wise man speak.

Best of all, this book comes from the heart of someone who has selflessly practiced what he has preached. I know you'll enjoy it as much as my teammates and I enjoyed Charles' message that July morning in Cleveland.

God bless you!

—*Orel L. Hershiser IV*
Orlando, Florida

PREFACE

This book is written for Christians who are making public declarations before audiences in any kind of circumstance. This includes Sunday school teachers, Bible study leaders, preachers, and teachers of preachers. In fact, I have written it for anyone who seeks to hold the attention of listeners.

Because we are so visually stimulated in almost any form of presentation today, getting and holding the attention of children or adults becomes more challenging. The simple truth is that listening comes from wanting to hear. Listeners have to be caught and held.

Built into the chapters that follow are avenues of approach to catching minds and causing them to want to listen. That's never easy, but the Word must be heard and heeded. Examples of communication from the Bible guide each chapter.

This book stands on many shoulders. Years of preaching, including teaching at Ashland Theological Seminary, have placed books and ideas before me in abundance. Out of those years have come chapters of experience in making people want to hear the Word.

One of my seminary students, Tom Petersburg, was the chaplain for the Cleveland Indians baseball team. It was his invitation to speak to the chapel service for the ball club that brought me in touch with Orel Hershiser.

The Foreword sets the scene for the making of this book. When Orel Hershiser, then pitcher for the Cleveland Indians, asked me whether I had ever written a book, I had to say that I had not. He asked me whether I would like to. This book is my answer and my thanks.

Pitcher Orel Hershiser brought the Wolgemuth & Associates agency into the process, which recruited the writing skills of Bill Butterworth. When I submitted my early pages, Bill was the one who said I was off the mark. At that point, Robert D. Wolgemuth's question centered my focus: "How do you do what you do?" Bill then gave me enormous help in shaping the structure of the book.

From Wolgemuth & Associates also came the help of Jennifer Cortez, who offered much advice and encouragement. S. David Garber, Herald Press editor, provided his kind understanding and editing skills. Finally, my daughter Bonnie critiqued what I wrote and also helped to shape the book. To all of the above, I express my deepest heartfelt gratitude.

I will be forever grateful to Orel Hershiser for his confidence that I could produce a Christian book on communicating the Word of God. The very fact that I truly felt "carried along" by the Lord is a memory that I will cherish into eternity.

—*Charles R. Munson*
  Goshen, Indiana

PART ONE

WHY IS EFFECTIVE SPEAKING IMPORTANT?

1

TRUTH

THE BOTTOM LINE OF SIGNIFICANCE

It was a truly memorable introduction to a speech. "I stock shelves at the local grocery store," Jack began his three-minute speech in a Public Speaking 101 class taught by a friend of mine. "I'm responsible for the soft-drink aisle. So I'm familiar with the wide variety of soda available to consumers these days."

With that, Jack took a deep breath and began to rattle off a list of options that was mind-boggling:

We stock—

- Coca-Cola
- Diet Coke
- Pepsi
- Diet Pepsi
- RC Cola
- Diet Rite Cola
- Dr. Pepper
- Diet Dr. Pepper
- Tab
- Pepsi Free
- Mello Yellow
- 7-Up
- Diet 7-Up

- Sprite
- Diet Sprite
- A & W Root Beer
- Diet A & W
- Mountain Dew
- Mr. Pibb
- Hires Root Beer
- Mug Root Beer
- Barqs Root Beer
- Slice
- Diet Slice
- Crush
- Diet Crush
- Squirt
- Diet Squirt
- Cherry Coke
- Cherry Pepsi
- Canada Dry Ginger Ale

Jack mentioned many more brands of soft drink, but my memory fails me. I do recall that after he recited the long list of names, he began a second long list of sizes:

You can get these soft drinks in—
- 12-ounce cans
- 12-ounce four packs
- 12-ounce six packs
- 12-ounce eight packs
- 12-ounce twelve packs
- 12-ounce sixteen packs
- 12-ounce twenty-four packs
- 1-liter bottles
- 2-liter bottles
- refundable bottles
- nonrefundable bottles

- 1-liter two packs
- 2-liter two packs
- 1-liter six packs

Jack sang out each item with a mesmerizing cadence. Before long, he had achieved the desired effect: we were weary of all the possibilities in the soft-drink aisle. Just when we were all starting to ask ourselves where this was going, he delivered the unexpected answer:

> I deal with so many types of soft drinks in so many different types of bottles and cans that it can be over-whelming. Sometimes it's just too much. I don't want to see any more soft drinks, for they don't really sat-isfy anyway. What do I want? I want it to stop. I want someone to say to me,

> Ho, everyone who thirsts, come to the *waters;*
> and you that have no money, come. . . . (Isa. 55:1a)

With that attention-getting introduction, Jack explained to his audience the plan of salvation. The offer of Christ's living water had never sounded so appealing to the group before him. All the competing brand-name soft drinks didn't attract us nearly as much as the thought of cold, sparkling water from a mountain stream. The contrast nailed down the point of the speech: God's truth prevails.

The truth of God is far more important and far more satisfying than anything else in the world. The speaker who delivers the Truth stands apart from all others.

The starting point for the communicator of biblical truth is that it truly is *biblical truth*. We're not selling apples or explaining quadratic equations; we are teaching the supreme truth found in the Word of God. We do need apples and quadratics; yet in the Bible we are dealing with the very words of the most holy Lord. All truth is God's truth, and we are specially privileged to handle the pages of Scripture.

We want success in our attempt to communicate God's truth. We want to become the most effective communicators possible.

There are three types of speakers:

1. Those you can listen to, with difficulty.
2. Those you can't listen to at all.
3. Those you can't help but listen to because they are so genuine.

We all know people who fit into one of these three classes. By the way, I love things grouped in threes. It reminds me of the one-liner:

ONLY THREE THINGS IN LIFE ARE FOR SURE: DEATH, TAXES, AND SHIPPING-AND-HANDLING.

I hope that made you smile. I love things that make us laugh. Throughout the book, I'll be highlighting some of my favorite humor.

In which of these speaking groups do you find yourself? Would you like to move into that third group, those to whom *you can't help but listen*? That is the group that most effectively handles the Truth.

You can join the select group. That's what this book is all about.

1. THOSE YOU CAN LISTEN TO

These are the speakers who elicit the response, "Oh, he was okay." "She was nothing out of the ordinary, but it was all right." These kinds of reactions are better than nothing, but they certainly are not speakers "in demand."

Three traits characterize this type of speaker:

1. Enthusiasm is low.
2. Color is not bright.
3. Urgency is lacking.

Low enthusiasm is better than no enthusiasm, but not much. You want to pay attention to this speaker, but you have to work at it. Maybe it's a lecture in a classroom, and you're paying attention because you know you'll be tested on the material. But if it were in a setting where there were no exams, little would stick with you.

Maybe the speaker is afraid to talk in front of an audience. In the next chapter we'll see what God told Jeremiah about being timid and afraid of an audience; that word can help all of us.

Second, speakers you can listen to have a degree of *color* in their speaking, but not much. By color, we mean adding shades of tone and feeling to highlight the Truth. If the speech were being recorded on a heart monitor at a hospital's intensive care unit, color would cause it to register more than just a flat line. There would be a steady rise and fall on the screen.

Another way to brighten the color is through the use of mental pictures, such as metaphors. Thus Jesus sent a message to Herod: "Go and tell that fox" (Luke 13:32).

WHAT IS A METAPHOR?
IT IS FOR THE COWS TO GRAZE IN!

If such speakers hang only a few pictures on the walls of your mind, they are okay at best. Yet they need a powerful boost of imagination and creativity, as discussed in chapters 5 and 6 of this book (pages 75-100).

Third, those you can barely listen to are lacking in *urgency*. These speakers don't sound as though they believe what they're saying. Such salespersons wouldn't even buy their own product.

This is a critical matter. If people have to work hard to stay with the speaker in a Christian meeting, it is the Truth that takes the hit. The Word of God is diminished. The apostle Paul understood the importance of this matter, saying to the Corinthian believers:

> Therefore, knowing the fear of the Lord,
> we try to persuade others; . . .
> For the love of Christ urges us on,
> because we are convinced that one has died for all;
> therefore all have died. (2 Cor. 5:11, 14)

DID JESUS NEED TO SUFFER AND DIE ON THE CROSS FOR THIS SERMON TO BE PREACHED? (GRACIA GRINDAL)

How convinced are you? Does it show up in your speaking? If so, you will move from this class to those to whom you can't help but listen. But before we look at that elite group, there's another category of would-be communicators to consider.

2. THOSE YOU CAN'T LISTEN TO

Sadly, this is an easy group to identify. We all know someone who fits this description. I hope it's not true of you or me.

Three characteristics define this speaker:

• There is no light.

- There is no fire.
- There is no point.

No light. God spoke light into the world. Jesus came, bringing another kind of light—himself. He is the Light of the world (John 1: 9). The person who can't be listened to brings no enlightenment at all. For them, God's light does not come through brightly.

Our purpose as communicators is to illuminate others. God has spoken light. It is our responsibility to draw attention to that light from God, thus illuminating the audience.

When a person can't listen, it is because what is being offered makes no impression. It doesn't bring anything from "Way Back Then" to brighten today. We feel centuries away. We have no sense that "[God] has spoken *to us* by a Son" (Heb. 1:1-2).

It is not fair for us to let the Bible remain old. When we present it as ancient dust, there is no light for today. This situation is not what God had in mind. We need to build strong, easy-to-cross bridges. One cannot listen to a person who doesn't accept that responsibility in our modern world.

> SOMEONE SAID OF A SPEAKER,
> "THE ONLY WAY HE COULD HAVE SAID LESS
> WOULD HAVE BEEN TO HAVE TALKED LONGER!"

Second, we can't listen to speakers who have *no fire*. I heard a story about a church catching fire; it drew a crowd. The pastor asked one observer why he had come now to observe this tragedy, though he had never visited the church before. He replied, "The church has never been on fire before!"

People will pay attention if the speaker is on fire.

Such speakers don't bury their feelings and emotions deep down inside. Instead, they process their feelings, own them, and let them emerge. Before you draw a line in the sand on the ever-present controversy of emotion in preaching, here is one thing to remember:

Some excitement on the part of the speaker has to be present to guarantee any sort of hearing from the audience. Without excitement, we're back to the flat line.

Third, poor speakers make *no point*. When there is no point, we are dealing with a rambling rose. Rambling is as wearisome to an audience as anything else of which we can think.

The problem centers around a lack of organization. The speaker's road map has been glued together, and the states are not in order. Maine and Florida are together, as are Georgia and California. Orderly travel is impossible.

What's the purpose of the talk you're giving? That question is never addressed by a person you can't listen to. But speakers to whom you can't help but listen, ask and answer that question of purpose early in their preparation. In part 2 of the book, we talk a great deal about keys for properly preparing a presentation.

Finally, here's the group we've been waiting to meet.

3. THOSE YOU CAN'T HELP BUT LISTEN TO

This is the group we all want to join. Such teachers and speakers are crystal clear. That has much to do with why we can't help but listen. They are the personification of a punchy ad I recently saw in the newspaper for a Broadway musical:

NOTHING HAS EVER HELD YOU LIKE THIS.

Now that's the kind of speaker I want to be.

Three descriptions sum up why a speaker can hold you like that:

- They wrap the Truth in handsome clothing.
- They keep the Truth current.
- They send the Truth home and to work.

Such presenters understand the awesome privilege and responsibility of teaching the Word of God. They realize the Truth is what sets us free.

They present the Truth in a structure that puts it in the brightest light. They dress it up in new, handsome *clothes*. Their speech adorns the Truth and sets it off in just the right way. It glorifies God.

Another part of the picture is that the Truth is seen in *current* ways. In the preparation process, hold the Truth in one hand and the newspaper in the other. Keeping up with the times is crucial to being heard.

Third, these speakers send the Truth *home and to work*. This is all about application. Presenting the Scripture in a way that is practical will always make the message memorable; the audience will be taking it with them and using it!

Thus they bring God to the bottom line of our lives. They take the Word of God and put it into the depths of our hearts. They use it. Those are the speakers we want to be around. We all want to be such speakers. It can happen.

WHERE WE'RE GOING IN THIS BOOK

We want to be speakers you can't help but listen to. The truth of God deserves our very best. There are certain issues that these speakers all have in common, even though their individual styles may vary.

The starting point is *overcoming our initial fears* of public speaking. There is a wonderful passage of Scripture that gives us real encouragement to overcome this all-too-common malady (chap. 2).

Then (in part 2) we offer a breakdown of *the preparation process*. The beginning place is the Word of God. We will discuss how to find the right passage from which to speak, as well as an overview of the inductive Bible study process (chap. 3).

Structure is the next issue (chap. 4). Why do some teachers captivate us, while others leave us wanting? Many times we find the answer in the structure they have chosen for their teaching. The most effective structure is the one most easily remembered; we discuss how to make that happen.

To move teaching beyond the predictable, we need to take a look at bringing *imagination* into our presentations (chap. 5). This topic will be a key to personalizing our approach to speaking; each of us has a unique approach to creativity.

Teaching that comes to life maximizes *visual images* (chap. 6). Just as Jack walked us through the soft-drink aisle of his grocery store, we need to tap into visuals to help us communicate a deeper understanding of the Truth. We want to engage as many of our senses as we can.

One of the most helpful additions to a presentation is the proper use of *humor* (chap. 7). We examine the appropriate uses of humor in our teaching, as well as how to find things in life that are funny.

What about the actual *delivery* of the speech? The key to an effective delivery is learning to *be yourself* while in front of folks (chap. 8). We talk about how to develop your own effective presentation technique.

Public speaking is nothing more than an enlarged conversation. We believe the *conversational approach* will greatly improve your speaking, if you are not already using it (chap. 9).

How do you know if the audience is with you? We examine how to gain *attention* in our speaking (chap. 10). This includes how to read an audience, how to dialogue with them, how to handle interruptions, and a host of other practical issues related to the subject.

Body language can work for you or against you; we need to take a closer look at how it can help in our presentations (chap. 11). Since gestures, facial expressions, and body language make up 93 percent of our overall communication, this is a topic worth considering.

One particularly creative delivery style is through the use of *drama* (chap. 12). I have had some wonderful experiences with drama that involves the audience with the Scriptures and people with each other. I am anxious to pass my excitement along to you!

We conclude the book with a *self-examination* (chap. 13). I firmly believe that who you are is much more important than how well you speak. It is the personal fire in your heart that ultimately communicates the truth of God from person to person.

Are you excited? Are you nervous? Are you a combination of the two? Well, relax, my friend. Let's take some time to talk together about fear. We all experience it. Everyone has dealt with it in one way or another.

God knows we have fears. He has some great advice for us on how to overcome them. Let's check out God's counsel.

FEAR

OVERCOMING COMMON FEARS IN SPEAKING

Fear.
I can vividly remember when darkness descended with the beginning of World War 2. President Franklin Roosevelt, sensing how frightened we had become, calmed the nation with the now-famous words,

WE HAVE NOTHING TO FEAR BUT FEAR ITSELF.

Here is a hint worth considering: some of our fear is positive in nature; the negative part almost always has to do with insufficient preparation! God directly addressed the issue of fear on numerous occasions in his Word. Let's consider a choice passage found in the Old Testament book of Jeremiah.

THE BIBLE SPEAKS ABOUT FEAR

Nothing hinders us from proclaiming the Word of God more than the fear to speak it out. Whether it's speaking one to one, or one to a hundred, lack of self-confidence and fear create unhealthy limitations on the speaker. Timidity in the air is stifling.

For Christians, we need to take hold of President

Roosevelt's words. But there is an even more important lesson against fear that God himself presented to the prophet Jeremiah.

Jeremiah protested about God's assignment for him. He claimed to be too young and added that he was not able to speak. This all sounds like excuse time in Public Speaking 101.

But God spoke to Jeremiah and took care of his fear and timidity:

> Do not say, "I am only a boy";
> for you shall go to all to whom I send you,
> and you shall speak whatever I command you.
> Do not be afraid of them,
> for I am with you to deliver you. (Jer. 1:7)

God kept his promise. Jeremiah became one of God's servants—a prophet. God gave him words and rescued him from death at the hands of people who became enemies because of those words (Jer. 38:6-10).

If we are to tame the lion of fear within, we must learn to appropriate the principles involved in how the prophet became so outspoken. He literally became *new*.

Let's hold in our view the amazing transformation that overcame the timid prophet. From his experience, we will find help for us poor souls who are not prophets but timid Christians.

The recast prophet seems to have been made over immediately, but we cannot be certain of that. Whenever it happened, God put iron in his soul. Let's look more closely at the dialogue between the Lord and the prophet.

> *Jeremiah:* Truly I do not know how to speak,
>   for I am only a boy. . . .

God: You, gird up your loins;
    stand up and tell them everything
       that I command you.
   Do not break down before them,
   or I will break you before them.
   And I for my part have made you today
    a fortified city,
      an iron pillar,
        and a bronze wall,
against the whole land. (Jer. 1:6, 17-18)

Orders have to be communicated clearly so they can be followed specifically. God did just that. We see in this passage three principles, three ways to wall out fears:

- Believe in God and act as if.
- Get yourself ready, stand up, speak up.
- Picture yourself safe inside a walled city.

Let's look at each of these three pieces of counsel.

BELIEVE IN GOD AND ACT AS IF

This is the surest faith highway to travel if we are going to overcome fear. It worked for the prophet, and it can reconstruct our thinking, giving us calmness in place of fear.

We cannot be sure exactly how the words came to the prophet. We only know that he believed in the reality of God, he was not afraid to speak, and the security wall around him was so vivid that he could speak without fear of the consequences. That didn't keep him from complaining, as we shall see.

APPEARING BEFORE AN AUDIENCE CAN BE
GROUNDS FOR SEPARATION. WE WANT TO BE
SEPARATED FROM THE FRIGHTENING
AUDIENCE IN FRONT OF US!

That was exactly the feeling of the prophet. Jeremiah wanted out of the assignment. Apparently he didn't recall that Moses much earlier had tried to avoid speaking out and didn't get away with it. God even reminded Moses who had made his mouth! (Exod. 4:10-11).

Both Moses and Jeremiah pleaded the Old Testament version of the Fifth Amendment: "I refuse to speak on the grounds that it might incriminate me. If I speak, I'll be in trouble with the law of the land" (cf. Exod. 3:11-12; Jer. 1:19).

Their real feelings also come through: "I refuse to speak because I can't speak!" That's strange, isn't it? Two God-chosen leaders pleading incompetence! Their circumstances are different from ours. But are the reasons for not wanting to speak any different?

Do we fear failure? What will I look like up front if I bomb out? The ego says, "Don't risk failure; it's not worth it. The task is too monumental. I can't speak in front of that large audience, I can't teach that class, I can't lead devotions"—or whatever our situation might be.

Have you ever considered how this fear reflects on the Lord? I hope you don't think God would ever say, "I made you, but you are not intelligent enough to be in front of an audience."

Jeremiah tried thinking that way, but God would have none of it. Instead, the Lord told him that words would be provided: "Now I have put my words in your mouth" (Jer. 1:9). What could poor Jeremiah do? God always works with those who are willing; this prophet became willing.

No one wants to admit being ignorant, but fear really does come out of ignorance, not having the experience to know what you can do—and even more than that, what *God* can do through you. If you have no firsthand knowledge of how capable you are in speaking, then you have uncertainty, and that uncertainty is spelled F-E-A-R.

Jeremiah believed in God and acted that way. God hasn't gone into seclusion. He still helps people speak his words. When Jeremiah realized that God was supplying him authority and the words to speak, he went for it. He became fearless. The confidence came flooding in as Jeremiah acted "as if" he could do it—with God.

I saw a report about an acting cast preparing for a movie. They went to the site where the film was to be shot. It was an old house, and they all moved right in! They cooked the same food in the same way as the people they were to portray. They stayed in the house overnight, just like the people did in the story.

Then in the morning, they went to rehearsal. One actor commented, "We acted as if . . ." To depict the people in the story, they acted as if they were actually those people. They gained confidence from acting as if.

If you have the right stuff, you can act confident. If you don't, acting won't do you much good. However, studies have proved that acting self-confident and courageous will actually suppress fears and nervousness. It works.

Take a deep breath, a good full one. Look at the audience, those lovely faces out there. Tell yourself, "We all need to hear what is going to be said here today." Stretch your body as straight as you can. Think confidence, act as if you already have it, and you will be amazed at the results.

You should squarely face that audience you fear. During a horrible blizzard, a farmer went outside to observe his cattle in the fields. He made one important observation: all the cattle were facing into the storm. Whatever the meaning of that setting, the application ought to be clear: face the fear with the full confidence of words coming from God.

Think about this scene: Jeremiah was timid and weak-kneed, lacking in self-confidence, making excuses, and wanting out. When Jeremiah concluded that God was real, that he had been tapped on the shoulder to speak, he acted as if. He began to speak. Sure enough, the words came, and the confidence followed to make him bold.

Be assured that fear of an audience is not unique to you. Even famous people, well known for being in front of crowds, have admitted to their fears of appearing in public to speak. But also be assured, they overcame their fears.

As believers, we are not simply talking about ordinary public speaking. When God is in the details of the life of the speaker, that makes a profound difference. The Lord is in every issue of the life of youth workers, children's workers, and Bible study leaders. God is always in direct communication with those who are willing to listen to him.

There is an energy that comes to people who grasp the reality of God being "there for you." Thoughts and words come flying by, and you can take hold of them. Please don't misunderstand: this is not to be confused with merely winging it. This is a fuller, deeper comprehension of Immanuel, "God with us" (Jer. 1:8; Exod. 3:12; 4:12).

The excitement resulting from being in front of an audience will bring inspiration and even unexpected help. Add the dimension of "God with us," and there is a sense of purpose unlike any other.

Does that mean that all nervousness will be gone forever? As the kids say, "Get real." It is important to realize that some worry keeps one on an edge that is sharp and helpful. It cuts away the ego that would lead you to think you did it all by yourself.

There are motivational speakers touring around who

can help anyone do better, but our motivational speaker is God himself. We are helped with words from the Word. That's a winning combination.

Some preachers have been so bold as to suppose that the Holy Spirit would supply words to offer their congregation without their own preparation. That's like a self-made man; one can tell right away that God had nothing to do with the making. If a speaker opens the Bible randomly and trusts the Spirit to lead him, we all will likely know before long that the Spirit had nothing to do with the sermon.

The Lord is looking for people willing to say, "I believe you, God. I am willing to take responsibility for teaching the class"—or for whatever the assignment may be. So you say yes to the challenge, act as if you can accomplish it, and prepare; like the prophet, you will be transformed. The more you say yes, the more your knees will stop knocking. God will be there for you.

There is a second principle at work in defeating fear:

Get Ready, Stand Up, Speak Up

The text of Jeremiah puts it this way:

Get yourself ready! Stand up and say . . . (1:17, NIV)

To a Hebrew, getting ready meant gathering up the long outer garment in preparation for walking or running. "Gird up your loins" (1:17). Thus Jeremiah would prepare to "go" and speak authoritatively to a rebellious people, like those around Jeremiah (2:2).

Let's break down these three components.

Get Ready

If you are going to be in front of an audience, the challenge before you is to be prepared; preparation is a major part of gaining confidence. It is all about understanding that "God is here for me." Take our word for it: that understanding will get you through!

An outstanding confidence-builder lies in the knowledge that you have something to say. Getting ready is the key to unlocking the door of your willingness to stand up and speak for the Lord.

Much of our fear comes from that frightening thought of *failing* in front of others. Preparation does away with that fear; there's no reason to feel that nervousness since you are wonderfully prepared in advance to go out in front of the crowd and communicate with them.

Conquering fear reminds me a great deal of learning how to swim. Sometimes you just have to *jump in!*

A LITTLE BOY WENT TO HIS FIRST SWIMMING CLASS. THE TEACHER ANNOUNCED, "ALL OF YOU WHO CAN SWIM, JUMP INTO THE DEEP END. IF YOU CANNOT SWIM, GO TO THE SHALLOW END."

THE BOY RAN TO THE DEEP END, JUMPED IN, FLOUNDERED ABOUT WILDLY, AND ALMOST DROWNED.

THE INSTRUCTOR PULLED HIM OUT AND SCOLDED, "I SAID, 'IF YOU CAN'T SWIM, GO TO THE SHALLOW END.' WHY DID YOU JUMP IN THE DEEP END?"

THE BOY REPLIED, "WELL, I DIDN'T KNOW IF I COULD SWIM OR NOT!"

Nothing can match the confidence that accompanies being ready. We are devoting all of part 2 in this book to preparation; it is that important.

We've seen the Lord communicate the need for preparation to the Old Testament prophet Jeremiah. Here's another passage to consider, this one from 1 Peter in the New Testament:

> Now who will harm you if you are eager to do what is good? But even if you do suffer for doing what is right, you are blessed. Do not fear what they fear, and do not be intimidated, but in your hearts sanctify Christ as Lord. *Always be ready to make your defense to anyone who demands from you an accounting for the hope that is in you;* yet do it with gentleness and reverence. Keep your conscience clear, so that, when you are maligned, those who abuse you for your good conduct in Christ may be put to shame. (3:13-16)

We ought to be obsessed with discovering what we believe and why we believe it. This is not a matter of preparing to debate but to give "an accounting." That's a big difference.

We have no knowledge of the preparation God had in mind for the prophet Jeremiah. Surely we can assume, however, that getting ready always requires opening up to God first. This is a deeper plunge than accepting the reality of God. This is seeing by faith that God is alive and well, and that he will give me light both in expected and unexpected ways.

This light may come in quiet moments of prayer and meditation. Or maybe on the street, in a car, in the woods, as we are always open to our heavenly Father touching our minds. We should expect "encounters of the God kind." They bring guidance and help.

Stand Up

Don't you wonder how the prophet heard the instruction to get ready and stand up? Was it in a dream or a vision? Or did God himself shout from heaven?

The order is clear: "Stand up." No matter how we feel about fear, this command is straightforward. Standing up is proper and in accord with building up confidence. As we so often hear in the sports arena, just do it.

We've always found it amusing when someone says, "But I can't think standing up!" Can God help us only when we're sitting down? Does all the blood rush from our heads when we stand?

Why did God tell the prophet to stand? Was it to give Jeremiah a view of himself actually standing before the people? Was it so he could gain actual confidence and minimize his fear? Was it to stir up his energy? Was it so he would be noticed and heard? These are possibilities.

God knew there would be fears and nervousness; that is why he told Jeremiah to "get ready and stand." Just to think of standing in front of a group strikes fear in the hearts of many.

Nevertheless, this is an order from God. And Jeremiah stood up. The message is clear. Imagine God pointing his finger at you, like Michelangelo's famous painting on the Sistine Chapel. He wants something of you.

Imagine that you have been walking past a building and have seen smoke rising out of it. You have come running into the building, shouting "Fire, fire!" at the top of your lungs.

The people inside need to hear what you have to say, right? Yet what you have to say from God's Word is even more important than sounding a fire alarm.

Speak Up

Tell them everything that I command you. (Jer. 1:17)

We're not merely talking about being loud enough to be heard. This is about *the Truth* being heard. Cotton candy will not bring the good news to life. The big ball of fluff will dissolve in moments. What is offered in speeches is often sweet to the taste and accepted, but it just doesn't stick to the ribs.

Fear often keeps us from speaking, as we have seen. But it may also hold us back from saying what might touch nerves and cause knee-jerk reactions. The people may need tough, nerve-tingling preaching and teaching. But don't forget Peter's counsel: "Do this with gentleness and respect" (1 Pet. 3:15b, NIV).

Speaking up is an urgent matter for Christ's new creations (2 Cor. 5:17). Why don't we have a compelling urge to do this? Complacency takes its toll from us. But Jeremiah had a calling from God, something he had to do. Jeremiah paid a personal price for his obedience; we may not want to consider the cost. Jeremiah complained,

> O Lord, you deceived me, and I was deceived. . . .
> Whenever I speak, I cry out
>   proclaiming violence and destruction.
> So the word of the Lord has brought me
>   insult and reproach all day long. (20:7-8, NIV)

This reminds us of the words of Jesus: "Count the cost" (cf. Luke 14:27-28; 9:23-26). There is a price to pay for effectively communicating God's truth, but the gain is worth the price. Here's a final way to protect yourself:

PICTURE YOURSELF IN A WALLED CITY

As we emphasize over and over in this book, we are strong believers in the use of *pictures* in speaking. There is nothing like a good visual image to reveal the meaning of something. Jeremiah made his defense for not wanting to speak to anybody about anything. But God told him that things were going to be otherwise. To calm any nervousness, God promises Jeremiah protection like that of a walled city (1:18).

Unless you have been overseas and seen a walled city like Jerusalem, it is difficult to imagine what God is promising. But Jeremiah knew. A walled city probably conjured up thoughts of the wall around Jerusalem. Some parts of that wall were forty feet thick at the bottom and twenty-five feet thick at the top. Sometimes cities were double-walled (as in 2 Kings 25:4). God told Jeremiah that his protection was a "bronze wall."

Since gates were the most vulnerable part of a wall, they were often covered with bronze. Sometimes sets of gates were offset: the enemy could not go straight in, but would have to break through one gate, turn, and fight at another gate to the right or left. Guard towers were built above all the gates, with guards ready to throw huge stones down on the enemy.

As Jeremiah envisioned this picture, the message from the Lord was clear: "Don't be afraid, for I have protected you behind these walls; fear is walled away from you!"

This is the Old Testament version of a modern American security system. Gated communities are popular today, as well as home security systems, car alarms, and the like.

The prophet Jeremiah needed a security system to overcome his fear. Such fear is real for all of us at some point in our lives. Fear can be beneficial when it enables us to be alert to danger. But audiences usually don't threaten any real danger. Therefore, we need to trust that God is taking care of us.

As you stand up to speak, imagine yourself in that walled city. You are protected. The protection is even more effective than forty feet of stone. You have God himself watching over you, guiding you in every word and phrase. Our speaking is all about yielding to God in everything we do, including our speaking. Fears are normal, but they don't need to paralyze us.

Remember the three key issues of this chapter:

- Assume the reality of God and act as if you can, with God.
- Get ready, stand up, and speak up.
- Picture yourself in a fortified city.

With those helpful attitudes in mind, let's move on to a more detailed development of the preparation process.

PART TWO

HOW DO I PREPARE TO SPEAK?

3

SCRIPTURES

THE STARTING POINT
OF TEACHING

Some Bible study groups use the Bible only as a symbol. They refer to it on occasion but do not use it as the base for teaching. Some preachers make glancing references to the Scriptures but not as the foundational element of their teaching. I recently heard of a pastor who boasted, "When I prepare a sermon, I don't read the Bible." We hope that pastor has read the Bible sometime!

How delightful it is that we can start with the Word of God. We want our teaching to be more than *about* Scripture; we want it to be *from* Scripture. The Bible is not only the starting point of our teaching; it is also the middle and the end. Children need to hear from it and to see it before them. Congregations need to know that the source of the words they hear is God's holy Word.

Group leaders often do not take preparation seriously; as a result, the Scripture is not the starting point or the ending point, but merely an assumed far-off reference point. Often they focus on the current needs of a group, going by popular assessment and the audience's age and status.

There is nothing wrong with stressing issues, but leaving the Bible out of a central position *is* wrong. People in such study classes may intend to be biblical, but they only assume use of the Bible and do not practice consistent Bible study.

Perhaps they neglect serious Bible study because the Bible appears to be difficult, and preparation takes time. It is much easier to use life-relevant articles and topics that can be assigned and brought into focus when the group meets. That procedure can be valuable. But if the Bible is not given its rightful place of authority, the class might just as well be a psychology class, an ethics forum, or a health dialogue in the town hall.

Scripture must be the starting point. If not, people are unconsciously led to think that the Bible is out-of-date.

What if there were *handles* on your Bible to help you lift it up to the place it rightly belongs? This chapter is designed to provide you with that very thing. We offer you ways to grip the Bible so you can raise up the Word for your group. This is an effective format to pilot you through the development of a biblical text and keep it as the primary source of your teaching.

Remember that getting yesterday's Bible story to fit into today's fax-paced world will require skill and hard work. Yet confidence will come as you develop these skills and apply them with diligence. Here is a way to start with the Bible and stay with it.

1. SELECT A SCRIPTURE

How do I find the right Scripture passage from which to speak? This is the top question, not an issue to be taken lightly. I want to know that God directs me to choose the right words.

Some teachers work through the Bible methodically, so their text is always clearly defined for each session. If they are teaching through 1 Peter, they may teach the first 12 verses of chapter 1 during the first session, verses 13-

25 during the second session, and so on.

What about the person who must decide on a text for each session, without the advantage of teaching through the Bible in a systematic way? Three elements come to mind as absolute necessities in this process of deciding:

- Prayer
- Reading
- Waiting

Right selection also results from a right understanding of the audience. Think about these questions:

- What occasion brings this group together?
- What is the average age?
- Will the people be in pews, chairs, around tables, or in a circle?
- What has preceded you on the program?
- What has preceded you in the recent weeks?

If you are regularly before the same group, many of these issues are already settled. But don't forget to carefully consider the group in its most current situation. What is going on in the community? What is going on in the world? This will always help you in selecting what God might want to say through you.

You may even have to lay the Bible aside after reading and do something else in order to find the right Scripture. The interval often provides your subconscious with time to work and God with time to provide. God is in the details. But for God to work in the details, you need to start your preparation early.

Locating the right portion of Scripture requires patience and diligence in the search process. We are not dealing with ordinary material but with the Word of God. The leader must first hear that Word at the right time and with the right spirit to communicate it effectively to the listeners.

2. DEVELOP AN IDEA SHEET

Once you have selected the portion of Scripture you feel God wants you to use, you are now ready to begin writing down ideas as you read the text over and over. Don't worry about the right order in your notes, or whether sentences are complete. Your goal is simply to *identify ideas*.

In this way you are getting acquainted with the text. You are making friends, meeting the people, places, and things described in the passage. Enjoy the excitement of these new friends and surroundings in the best thought environment in the world!

Don't quit too soon; friends aren't usually made quickly. The random ideas you hold on paper will contribute later to your development of the Scripture passage. You will be tempted to think, *I must hurry through this part of the process, so I can get on to the finished product.* But given enough time, the ideas gathered will be a valuable resource in the total process of understanding.

A real advantage to this system is that even when you must leave your study, you can take your idea sheet with you. With God in the details, you never know when there will be a flash of light while you are running an errand or waiting for someone or even while you are driving.

> **CAUTION: WRITING WHILE DRIVING COULD BE HAZARDOUS TO YOUR HEALTH.**

A Sunday school teacher may come to a great idea while taking care of children at home, or in the produce aisle of the neighborhood grocery store. Always be ready to receive insight and to record it promptly.

Finding the right Scripture and writing down your ideas are crucial steps to becoming confident and competent. After doing that, we can move on to further development of the chosen passage.

3. DETERMINE THE BOUNDARIES

At this point there is no certainty on how broad or how narrow you need to go in your study. The goal is saturation—probing, asking questions, getting a feel for what is in front of you, being awed by the fact that God is dealing with all of humankind through the Book on your lap, and believing that he will use you to communicate his message.

We are not yet discussing sermon development or a class presentation. This step is about setting boundaries on the passage of Scripture. It is important to try to determine the framework of the biblical writer's thoughts. What group of verses make up a unit of thought in the passage? That is an important question to answer, so much so that we need to define exactly what is meant by unit of thought.

> *Unit of thought:* The number of paragraphs it takes to complete a thought; that which constitutes the beginning and ending of the author's thought unit.

For example, 1 John 2:28—3:10 is a unit of thought inside the broader subject of the entire letter of John the apostle.

Now, having defined boundaries as a unit of thought, what is inside? What is the heart or core, the single chief thought?

4. FIND THE CORE UNIT OF THOUGHT

What do we mean by *core?*

Core: That around which everything orbits;
the heart that beats inside the unit of thought.

In our example of 1 John 2:28—3:10, the heart that beats inside these paragraphs is the phrase *children of God.* This is the *core idea* of the entire *unit of thought.*

In some Bible editions, added notes provide such information. The boundaries are already determined, and the heading is already printed over the *unit of thought.* If that is the case, don't be tempted to skip through this item quickly. Can *you* determine why that particular core was chosen? Until you can, your work on this step is not completed.

In the example passage from 1 John, the core *(children of God, or child of God)* is found in 3:10. What John is talking about in these paragraphs is the *core idea (children of God, child of God).* So everything revolves around that phrase. You can fence in those paragraphs under that one heading. Then you might decide to use 3:1-10 as your text, choosing to develop those key paragraphs.

Thus far we have given attention to finding the Scripture, writing down our ideas from reading, finding the *unit of thought,* and getting to the *core idea.* Let's press on.

5. IDENTIFY WHAT THE BIBLICAL WRITER IS SAYING ABOUT THE CORE IDEA

If the *core idea* or heart of the five paragraphs is *children of God,* what is John *saying* about that? When John talks about *children of God* in 2:28—3:10, what is he saying about those children?

At this point, we can return to our *idea sheet* developed in step 2. We have gathered and written down ideas from reading and rereading the passage. All these notes can help determine what John is saying. It won't be everything, but it's the ideal starting place.

Here's an example to consider:

3:10   John is talking about *children of God.* (core idea)

2:28—3:10   John is saying this about *children of God.* (unit of thought)

2:28   Little children, abide in God. (NIV paragraph)

2:29   Children are born of God. (NIV par.)

3:2   Children will be like God. (NIV par.)

3:4   Jesus takes away our sin. (NIV par.)

3:10   Children of God, do right and love. (NIV par.)

Note that each paragraph (in NIV) has its own core and could be developed as much as desired. At this stage, we're just trying to get the big picture, not developing an outline for presentation. The next chapter handles that.

So in steps 3-5, we have scouted out boundaries that fence in a single *unit of thought,* identified what John is talking about *(core idea),* and traced what John is saying about that single *unit of thought.*

What is the writer talking about? What is he saying about what he is talking about? These are two important questions to keep in mind at all times. Now we need to tap some additional help.

6. SURF THE TESTAMENTS

Allowing the Bible to speak for itself is one of the best tools available for Bible study. You can roam through the Testaments anytime, but the best time is after some basics have been accomplished. I like it in this position because we have already read and reread the selected text, and written down ideas from it.

Regular surfing can also be part of building confidence because afterward you know you have done your homework. Check far and wide to obtain the most valuable assistance you can find.

You will find valuable support from any source that leads you to other helpful portions of the Bible. Commentaries, theology books, concordances, and Bible dictionaries should be used. But don't allow them to supplant the Bible's own resources.

Let's return to our sample text in 1 John to see the value of surfing. Suppose you are an adult leader in some teaching capacity working through 1 John 2:28—3:10. A concordance will help you realize you have at least *forty-six* cross-references to assist you in your preparation.

> *Example:* 2:28 uses the word *confidence.* You can get help in understanding that word from Ephesians 3:12; you may be referred to 2:18 for more help on *access.*

> *Example:* 3:9 says that no one born of God will continue to sin. Psalm 119:2-3 offers help:
> Happy are those who keep his decrees,
>   who seek him with their whole heart,
> who also do no wrong,
>   but walk in his ways.

Surfing the Testaments is like surfing the Internet. It can take you to endless sources of information.

DOES ON-LINE MEAN THAT THE CLOTHES ARE NOT DRY?

After we have accomplished these six steps, we are ready to consider how the material is going to be transferred to the audience.

7. DISTILL THE MATERIAL AND WRITE A POWER STATEMENT

To transfer what you have studied to an audience, you need to distill the gathered material. You can't offer the group everything you've gleaned in your study. Hence, you need to boil it down to a concentrated summary.

From your whole package of notes, begin sorting out ideas, writing, and writing again until the process yields a few basic sentences. Keep reducing it until you have several boxes into which you can do your sorting.

Here are some examples from our brother John.

From the Scripture
- We do not know what we shall be. (3:2)
- We do know that when Jesus appears, we shall be like him.
- We do know that we shall see Jesus when he appears.
- We do know that with this hope, we shall be purified.

Developed out of the Scripture
- Children of God live and love like God.
- We know if we expect purity *then,* we must have purity *now.*
- We know that love and selfishness do not mix.
- We know that we must resist the devil.

The best way to bring all this data together is to develop a *power statement*. This is a summary statement, bringing everything to one all-inclusive sentence. You may need to write a dozen of them before landing on the right one, but it will be worth the effort. (By the way, don't discard the first eleven statements; it's possible they can be used later in the message's development.)

This developed statement becomes the *organizing principle* for anything you do publicly with the material. A well-thought-through sentence will guide you and keep you on track.

By constantly keeping in touch with the way you have summarized the whole package, you can help eliminate wandering (or at least keep it to a minimum).

A primary use for the *power statement* is to place it at the beginning of what you say to your audience. In that way, it is a contract or agreement with the people, a promise you are prepared to keep. You can use it during the delivery to remind you and the audience where you have been and where you are going.

Here are two examples of early attempts to summarize our sample text. The first one is broad, and the second is more inclusive:

Power statement 1
Children of God can't live like the devil.

This is a narrow summary of the section. You are either a child of God or a child of the devil. Essentially, John summarizes the passage that way as he closes the paragraph in 3:10.

Power statement 2
We are children of God because God washed us in love and in Jesus destroyed the devil's work; so if we continue to practice sin and refuse to love one another, we are orphans.

In a more definitive sentence, the second example covers the love of God, the work of Jesus, lawlessness and its continued practice, and finally deals with the refusal to love one another.

Almost nothing can shape you up better, or give you more confidence, than summarizing your entire train of thought into one sentence. You become sure that you have what you are going to say well in hand; that will put iron in your backbone.

8. LOCATE PICTURES IN THE SCRIPTURE ALBUM

There are pictures in everything you study in your Bible. Sometimes they are right out in front of you. Other times, they are like a hologram on a credit card: you can't see them until you turn the card a certain way. The images and pictures are there; you just have to learn how to turn the verse around in your mind so you can see it.

Seeing the Scriptures in pictures is a valuable wellspring of ideas. Seeing is relatively simple if one is geared to looking for pictures. If you're not wired that visual way, here's some help. *Linger with a word and draw a picture in your mind.* Consider these questions in our sample text in 1 John:

2:28   Can you see children of God who will be confident and unashamed at Jesus' second coming? How do these people look and act? Can you visualize his coming?

2:29   What picture do you get of doing right?

3:7   Can you see Jesus destroying the devil's work? How much do you see? Is it a vivid picture? What is the devil's work?

3:10   What does a child of the devil look like? Do

you get any images at all? Does any person come to mind?

Pictures are everywhere in the Bible, but to find them, we must be searching. Someone asked an earth scientist how he spent his summer. He replied, "I was only able to study half of my backyard." He meant that he had studied every blade of grass, every flower, every tree, and anything that flew, crawled, or slithered there. That is the diligence we must cultivate to see all that the Bible offers to us.

9. NOTCH OUT THE PASSAGE OF SCRIPTURE

The goal of this step is to reach the place where thoughts stand out and we exclaim, "I see what it means now!"

One method of doing this is to put three or four translations before you and write out the passage in your own words. By rearranging the text itself, being careful not to damage the content and intent, you are able to get ideas out into view for a closer look. The process stretches out the passage and gives you a clearer grasp of it.

Engaging in such an exercise develops great mental and emotional confidence for you. A creation process is going on because you are completely focused. You are lifting the ideas up and out, so you can examine them more carefully. The truth is not changed, but you can view it better as you have processed it in your mind and written it down.

The final result will make an impact on you. The effort of creating allows you to look inside and to think into the intent of the Scripture from the minds of several translators.

Another method to make thoughts stand out individually is to *notch the ideas*. Notching is stretching out the look of the passage so that you can better isolate the thoughts. Ephesians 1:16-23 is a written prayer by the apostle Paul. Notched out, it looks like this:

Here is my prayer:
        that the God of our Lord Jesus Christ,
        the glorious Father,

    may give you the spirit of wisdom,
    may give you the spirit of revelation,

      so that you may know him better,
      having the eyes of your heart enlightened,

    that you may know the hope of his calling,
    that you may know the inheritance promised
            to believers,
    that you may know the greatness of the power avail-
            able to believers,

    demonstrated in the resurrection of Jesus,
    demonstrated in the place of honor Christ has
            in heaven,
    demonstrated in the position Christ has as the Head
            of the church,

    his body,
        in which he fully lives. (paraphrased)

Notice how "that you may know" and "demonstrat-ed" are deliberately repeated so that each idea stands alone. Lifting out any one of those sentences provides substantial material for development. Circles or boxes can be drawn around significant words or ideas for further high-lighting.

When you read the passage this way and stretch it, or notch it out, you may find great understanding and use-fulness. You have separated ideas that can stand alone, or you can join them in a new way. Keep notching or stretch-ing until all the thought is taken to its completion.

Every piece of the Bible can be stretched out. Some are more challenging than others, but it works for all types of Scripture. Here's an example from Mark 14:3-11, a nar-rative passage:

While Jesus was in Bethany,
> reclining at the table in the home of Simon the
> > leper,

> a woman came in
with an alabaster jar of very expensive perfume.
> She broke the jar;
> she poured the perfume on his head.

Some of those present
> were indignantly saying to one another,
> "Why this waste of perfume?
> It could have been sold for more than a year's wages.
> The money could have been given to the poor."
> > They rebuked her harshly.

Jesus said, "Leave her alone.
> Why are you bothering her?
> She has done a beautiful thing to me.

> "The poor you will always have with you.
> You can help them anytime you want.

"But you will not always have me.
She did what she could.
She poured perfume on my body
   to prepare for my burial."

Jesus said, "I tell you the truth.
   Whenever the gospel is preached
      throughout the world,
         what she has done
            will also be told
               in memory of her."

Then Judas Iscariot, who was one of the Twelve,
      went to the chief priests
   to betray Jesus
      to them.
         They were delighted to hear this.
         They promised to give him money.

Then Judas watched for an opportunity
      to hand him over. (paraphrased)

   Reading the passage with sentences individualized like this gives you an opportunity to pause and visualize the events of the story in a new form. The openness of the paragraphs gives the mind a new ability to see.

   You can pause with Jesus, watching the woman breaking the vial and pouring the perfume. You can imagine Judas looking for an opportunity to betray Jesus.

   You could have visualized it before. Yet a new form that you have created works double for you. First, as you create a new setting by isolating sentences, you latch onto ideas that may be fresh. Second, in reading your creation, there is another opportunity for insight.

10. DECIDE WHAT TRUTH YOU WANT TO TRANSFER FROM YOUR STUDY

You now need to use everything discovered thus far and make a determination: What truth do you want to pass on to your audience? Drawing from all that you have studied, how can you put it together in an order? Everyone needs a deep well from which to draw so that the Scripture is not hindered in its approach to people.

> **A YOUNG COLLEGE STUDENT DROPPED HER RING DOWN A WELL. SEVERAL YOUNG MEN VOLUNTEERED TO GO DOWN FOR THE RING, BUT SHE REFUSED THEM ALL.**
>
> **THEN ALONG CAME AN OLD COLLEGE PROFESSOR WHO OFFERED TO GO DOWN FOR THE RING, AND SHE SAID YES.**
>
> **"WHY DID YOU CHOOSE HIM OVER US?" THE YOUNG MEN ASKED.**
>
> **SHE REPLIED, "HE CAN GO DEEPER, STAY UNDER LONGER, AND COME UP DRIER THAN ANYONE I KNOW!"**

Now we have the contents ready for our package, but we still need to decide what kind of package to put it in. Think of these questions:

- What kind of box is needed?
- How shall I wrap the contents to avoid damage?
- Where is the package going?
- How is it going to get there?
- How will I recognize "destination achieved"?

These are questions the next chapter will answer.

This chapter has offered you ten handles to help you draw what you need from the Scriptures:

1. Select a Scripture.
2. Develop an idea sheet from reading that Scripture.
3. Find the boundaries by forming a *unit of thought*.
4. Find the *core idea*.
5. Identify what the writer says about the *core idea?*
6. Surf the Testaments.
7. Distill the material into a *power statement*.
8. Look for pictures in the Scripture album.
9. Notch out the passage.
10. Decide what truth you want to relay to your audience.

Do those ten steps seem like a lot of work? You're right—they are! You have to make a decision. How much time are you willing to spend in order to be ready for your listeners? How important is delivering words from God's Word? The material we have presented is merely a guide; it's your call on how involved you make it. But do take your responsibility with the Scripture seriously.

Now we are going to move on to structuring or packaging the material for delivery. It is an important and even urgent message, so we will be sending it by *Priority Mail*.

4

STRUCTURE

PUT TEACHING IN THE MOST EFFECTIVE CONTEXT

Structure is "that which is built." It means to build something. In this chapter we talk about building a structure that will hold together under the pressure of an audience and the nervousness of the builder.

We want to offer some guidelines for structuring delivery systems. These will be well constructed, orderly, and easily remembered by the speaker and the audience.

Structure builders always need to ask,

- What are we going to build?
- How are we going to build it?
- How will we know when our building is finished?

When the Winchester rifle manufacturer died, his wife, Sarah, went into a depression about her own death. When she did die, she left an unfinished house with enough material on hand to continue the building project for many more years. During 40 years of construction, she had been assembling a house with 150 rooms, 13 bathrooms, 2,000 doors, 10,000 windows, stairs that went nowhere, and much more.

Mrs. Winchester knew what she was doing, as outrageous as her plan was. She had a "spirit-guide" who told her that as long as she kept building her house, she would never die.

Our goal is more realistic. Mrs. Winchester wanted to stay alive; our goal is to help people know how to live. We have plans, and the plans tell us where we are going and how to get there. When we are finished, we know that we have arrived.

Every public presentation needs a structure that will support the speaker and draw the attention of the listeners. Every audience needs to be held, in this case, by a person with thoughts and words in good order.

Structure can be broken down into three parts:

- Beginnings
- Middles
- Endings

Within the three parts of the structure, we suggest two types of beginnings, middles, and endings.

BEGINNINGS: INTRODUCTION

So how shall we begin? Consider the introduction of a presentation as the porch; that's where you are just before you enter the house. The audience is the house, and they are waiting for you to come in. If you enter too rapidly, you may startle them. But on the other hand, if you linger too long on their porch, they may become tired of waiting for you and leave by the back door of their minds.

We dare not linger; the introduction must be sharp, clear, and engaging. With a good and confident appearance and an interest-catching introduction, the speaker has gone a long way to ensure continued involvement with the minds of the audience.

When days were not encumbered with faxes, e-mail, TV, and the general rush of things, an audience could tolerate a leisurely or even meandering introduction by the speaker. But no longer.

Inquiring minds want to know, and they want to know now.

When you are standing before a Sunday school class, a Bible study, or a congregation, you need to engage minds quickly. That way you may have inner assurance that they will stay with you. To gain that early attention, you must have an opening that is arresting, something that rivets the minds onto what is going to follow.

These concerns call you to concentrate on details and plan precise words in the opening sentences. Without such preparation, they will leave you out on the porch. Such strategy requires time and thought and the desire to begin your moments with the audience in a confident mood. When you start right, you give everyone a sense of expectancy for what is about to take place.

There is some wisdom in *planning the introduction last* and the conclusion first. In that case, the *power statement* or summary statement has already been worked out; thus you already have the beginnings of an introduction.

However, you should not depend completely on the *power statement* to capture the audience. Though the *power statement* hopefully introduces the subject, you need something more to attract immediate attention. Think ahead while you are preparing and ideas are beginning to form. Make note of possibilities for opening sentences.

You can achieve an attention-getting introduction through the use of *an object*. When you hold up a visual aid, if it is relevant, it can stimulate the people's desire to hear. Other suggestions are things related to *current events*, or anything *surprising*. Think in terms of *arousing curiosity* about what you are going to say, or about something special to listen for in the Scriptures.

Truths from the Bible deserve right and proper introductions. Think about the following questions:

- What have I discovered in my study that will gain immediate attention?
- How about a thought-provoking question?
- Did something just happen in town that would connect the people with the message?
- Any major events in the news?
- Is there a joke I could tell that relates to the subject?

Whatever you do, get off the porch and into the house before the people leave!

Introductions are meant to introduce. "Jay Leno, I would like you to meet Arnold Schwarzenegger." That's an introduction. But here's a better one.

The apostle Paul did not consider himself a trained speaker, yet he may have underestimated his own abilities. He certainly knew how to begin and get the attention of his audience at the "meeting of the Areopagus." Check Acts 17:22-32 (paraphrased below):

"In every way you are very religious."
What did the people hear? *A compliment.*

"As I walked around, I looked carefully at your objects of worship."
What did the people hear? *I am interested in you.*

"I even found an altar with this inscription, 'To an unknown god.'"
What did the people hear? *He really knows us.*

"What you worship as something unknown,
   I am going to proclaim to you."
What did the people hear? *That's interesting. Let's listen.*

"The God who made the world
   and everything in it . . ."
What did the people hear? *Oh, that includes us.*

With these attention-grabbing comments, Paul is off the porch and into the house. He wastes no time; he gets right to the heart of the matter. That's a good introduction.

As basic as it may sound, don't forget that introductions are supposed to introduce. Now let's look at another form of opening.

BEGINNINGS: ONCE UPON A TIME

"Once upon a time" is an uncomplicated beginning to a whole other delivery system. Immediate attention is guaranteed. Adults will be captured as well as children. Someone described a children's sermon as a message that adults can understand. It's almost as if the adults were not present, but they are paying attention to what is going on.

Here we are not talking about an illustration, a story told to throw light on a point. Instead, we have another way to structure the truth from Scripture in story form.

In the little town of Joppa, there lived a man, and . . . Immediately one is drawn into the story, just like "once upon a time." Finish either of those sentences. Add details of the people, places, and things; name the problems that need to be resolved. If you do this, your audience will be involved. For young and old alike, there is magic moving through the phrase *Let me tell you a story.*

The Lord sent Nathan to David. He came to him,
and said to him, "There were two men in a certain
city, the one rich and the other poor. The rich man
had very many flocks and herds; but the poor man
had nothing but one little ewe lamb, which he had
bought. . . ." (2 Sam. 12:1-3a)

Note how carefully Nathan builds up interest and sus-
pense. Stories are mind-catchers and mind-holders. How?
Because we all are anxious to know how the story turns
out. By nature we are curious beings.

Knowing that, God has filled the Bible with mind-
catching, life-changing truths that can help us. If our
responsibility is the oral communication of these truths,
we need to be engaging and interesting. "Once upon a
time" can do that.

For a speech, we do not need a long introduction, as
for a novel. Instead, consider weaving storytelling elements into teaching structures, to keep life in our speaking. We want our presentations to seem more like conversations with someone than like an oration.

It is not necessary to actually say "once upon a time,"
but it is valuable to think that way. "Let me tell you a
story" in your structure building will loosen up anything
you prepare.

Thinking "three points" for a sermon is natural for a
preacher; more often than not, the Scripture text miracu-
lously lends itself to that format. But it is easy for these
outlines to become stiff and rigid.

The master of using "once upon a time" to capture the
attention of his audience was the Lord Jesus. *A farmer
went out to sow his seed. . . . The kingdom of heaven is
like . . ."* (Matt. 13). That kind of beginning ought to be
in the thought process of every teacher.

In one school in China, children are learning to be journalists and photographers. In one instance, the class members began publishing their own newspaper. The teachers encourage them to let their imaginations run free. One young girl summarized it best: "There are no fixed patterns." How freeing that is to an individual!

"No fixed patterns" ought to be a part of everyone's structure building. Don't abandon organization, but take care to have a story running along with your outline.

"Once upon a time" is just the beginning; yet it can change the way you think about your management of ideas. Now let's move on to the heart of the structure, the middle.

MIDDLES: BODY

Since beginnings are introductions, then middles must be in between them and the endings. Introduction, body, conclusion—that is a format as ancient as Aristotle. Yet today it is still the best form of structuring.

RECENTLY SOMEONE OVERHEARD A MAN SAY, "THE ANCIENTS HAVE STOLEN MY BEST IDEAS!"

We are getting even; we're stealing the ideas of the ancients. The middle is the body of material in a speech.

We have chosen to use the term in its plural (middles) because we have two types of bodies to suggest. The middle for a talk is its body, while the middle for a story is its action. First, let's look at the body.

The middle is what the speaker has promised to talk about in the *power statement* and the *introduction*. You must keep your promise. Sunday school teachers, study leaders, and pastors should all be promise-keepers. That will happen if you give attention to organizing your thoughts.

Whoever delivered your letters today had the mail sorted before starting on the route. They did not put missives for New York in the Chicago box, at least not deliberately. Likewise, they did not sort mail for Main Street into the Mayflower Street box. Knowing the right boxes is critical for New York, Chicago, Main Street, and Mayflower Street.

Providing the right boxes for organizing thought is more crucial than sorting mail, as important as that is. A letter can be rerouted, eventually arriving at its destination. But you might not be able to retract an idea that lands in the wrong box. You will confuse yourself and the audience, and lose or weaken the intent.

So the boxes must be in order; what goes in the boxes must also be in order. Consider this example:

A letter to a house church from Paul has three category-boxes at the end of the section entitled "Rules for Holy Living." The three boxes are in Colossians 3:15-17, arranged as follows:

- Let the peace of Christ rule. . . .
- Let the word of Christ dwell. . . .
- Do everything in the name of the Lord. . . .

The introduction should have promised a development of these ideas, stating where we are going. The body must fulfill that promise. Here are three clear mail slots into which material can be sorted. The category-boxes are right there in the scriptural text, making easy reference points.

What can you place into the first category-box? Anything from the passage or relevant ideas, as long as the ideas fulfill the first promise: "Let the peace of Christ rule."

Only by constant reference to your promised development of "Let the peace of Christ rule" can you make certain that you are selecting appropriate ideas.

I. Let the peace of Christ rule.
    A. Peace of Christ must rule.
        1.
        2.
    B. Being members of one body, you were called to peace.
        1.
        2.
    C. Be thankful.
        1.
        2.

Now there are category-boxes inside the larger category-box. What will fit in those? First is your promise, and from that follow all the descending elements of the outline, filling out what you promised.

Does everything fit those promises? Only constant reference to the master promise will guarantee that you are fulfilling your pledge.

When you are satisfied with the sorting, start at the bottom of the third category-box. Ask yourself, "Does everything here belong here?" Go to the next box up (the second) and ask the same question, then to the first box, asking again if the ideas fit under this promise.

Also ask, "Are the bridges or connections proper between the category-boxes?" Finally ask, "Will all the categories be introduced by the introduction?"

Here is what you have done: You have made certain that the ideas under all your promises belong there. If the smaller boxes fit into the larger box, and if all three of the larger boxes fulfill the introduction, and if the introduction fits the title and/or topic—then you win! You are going to Disney World.

MIDDLES: STORY LINE

Our second middle relates to the second introduction. It is the action, the story line, or the plot for our intro that began "Once upon a time." It is simply a continuation of what has already begun:

There was a craftsman much in disfavor with his fellow countrymen. He was not a bad man, but his trade kept him out of town and near the water. In his tanning business, he worked with dead-animal skins and other smelly materials; because of that, the townsfolk did not want him around them. Hence, he lived near the water in Joppa.

But Simon the tanner was about to receive a famous guest who would stay with him for some time. The two men made strange companions. Jews did not favor the handling of dead animals, which is what Simon did. The work was defiling and made him ritually unclean.

The guest, a Jew, surprisingly did not seem to be bothered by Simon's trade. Maybe he even used some of those tanned skins. By coincidence, they were both called Simon, but the guest was also called the Rock.

The companionship began many years earlier, when they were boys. Simon stayed close to home, but Peter went on the road. Now he was back and famous. Joppa was not Peter's home, but he just knew Simon the tanner would still be there. He also knew he would be welcome in the tanner's home.

The tanning business and Simon the tanner were problems for many people in Joppa, but not for the Rock. He could handle prejudice—no problem. However, can he handle everything that is going to happen to him?

"Once upon a time" is now completed. The introduction is over, and you have set forth the *middle* or plot. People generally know what happened to Peter at Simon's home. Note, however, what can be done with a tiny verse of Scripture, just thirteen words:

[Peter] stayed in Joppa for some time with a certain Simon, a tanner. (Acts 9:43)

Add a little description to that:

[Peter] is lodging with Simon, a tanner, whose house is by the seaside. (Acts 10:6)

With those two brief clauses, you have the makings for an imaginary story with truth embedded and lessons to be learned.

There are several directions you can take. You can go backward and see what Peter has been doing in Joppa to make him famous. Or you can move forward and note what he is going to be doing in Caesarea. The last sentence of the above story opts for the forward route: "Can he handle everything that is going to happen to him?" There are still many options available.

From what has been introduced above, you can fill out the story by imagining how Peter and Simon became friends, and why Peter stayed with Simon. Other Jews would not like to board with a tanner. The story could turn on how prejudice develops and is overcome. Likely the tanner himself was a Jew, though practically an outcast.

There are so many details involved, and you should master all of them. But it is essential for you to select a few important ones. Think about the following details:

If You Visit Simon's House by the Sea—

- What sea is it?
- Do you see the water?
- What kind of house is it?
- Does it have a fence around it? (see 10:17).
- Have you checked out Acts 10:9?
- Can you see the two friends meeting?
- How long were they separated?
- Or were they not friends at all?

If You Visit Joppa—

- What kind of woman was Dorcas?
- What kinds of things did she make?
- Have you investigated her miraculous healing?
- Have you checked out the interesting conversations?

If You Visit Caesarea—

- Can you envision Peter's eating disorder?
- How big was the room where Peter spoke to his friends and the family of Cornelius?
- When Peter speaks of Jesus hanging on a tree, can you feel that?
- Can you feel the joy of the resurrection that Peter describes?
- Did Peter shout that part?

- Did he pause after stating it?
- How do you see what took place?

To develop the story, you can stay in Joppa, or go to Caesarea and visit with Cornelius; but you shouldn't do both. Soon we'll talk about ending the story.

Developing stories from Scripture is an excellent form to offer variety to your teaching. It is a great way to "loosen up" your teaching, moving from the stiffer introduction-body-conclusion form to an easier flow of ideas. Taking the stiffness out of the bones of an outline is so valuable. It's like a treatment with Ben-Gay ointment.

ENDINGS: CONCLUSION

A conclusion concludes; it draws the presentation to a close. Done properly, it will keep your message from a sudden or slow death. As mentioned earlier, there is some wisdom in preparing the conclusion first and the introduction last. In doing so, the preparer is forced to follow a focus or direction. This may well set the tone for the structure of the speech.

You should present the conclusion from a position of *strength*. Like a jockey with a racehorse, save some strength for the final effort. The conclusion should not needlessly linger. You don't want to offer a closing that whimpers to a stop.

Here are some questions to consider:

- What truth have you presented?
- What do you want the listeners to do about that truth?
- Have you suggested practical ways to appropriate that truth?
- Do you need to summarize those applications or offer them for other situations?

• What are you giving the people to take home?

The conclusion can say, "Here, take this with you. Here's how you can use it." Be sure not to offer anything new at this point. The time for new thoughts is over.

Often communicators pass by opportunities to stop without realizing it. The listeners will know it, thinking, *Should have stopped there!* Missing a suitable closing place results from a lack of planning.

Someone asked Ted Turner, CNN founder and billionaire, what he wanted on his tombstone. He replied,

I HAVE NOTHING MORE TO SAY.

For a tombstone, that's enough, but not for a conclusion to a speech. Beginnings and endings are the most difficult parts of structuring and delivering oral material. Doing either one gracefully takes serious preparation.

Think of it this way:

• The audience will remember little of what you say.
  Hence, your last words must be carefully crafted.

ENDINGS: RESOLUTION

How shall we bring resolution to our story of Simon's guest, the Rock? Shall we go to Joppa or Caesarea? Do we want to pursue the friendship between Simon and Peter? Or go on with Peter meeting Cornelius and his friends? Is the issue of prejudice a viable option? We must decide, for only one resolution works per story.

Obviously the resolution to our story depends on a fuller development of the plot. However, a resolution, unlike a conclusion, does not have to bring finality. In fact, a story has the luxury of allowing the hearers to make the resolution. The endings are not likely to be the same, but we all take different ideas from anything we might hear together.

So what shall we do with Peter? Taking him out of Joppa, especially to a town like Caesarea, provides endless possibilities. Going there was the Big Time. We also want to remember our leading question: "Can he handle everything that is going to happen to him?"

> The Rock didn't waver. He was with people who welcomed him warmly as a friend, but they were Gentiles. He was not even supposed to be in the house of a Gentile. But there he was, speaking boldly about Jesus being hanged and then raised.
>
> Even as he spoke, the Holy Spirit came on them all. "Even on the Gentiles," his astonished Jewish brothers said. Peter did not hesitate. He asked, "Can anyone keep these people from being baptized?" Then he ordered his friends to baptize the Gentiles "in the name of Jesus."

The beauty of stories is that they involve their hearers. The use of conversation and description are almost certain to make people want to hear more.

Our promise was to provide material to help you build your teaching structure. We offered ideas on moving from introductions to outlines, and from introductions to stories. Then we proposed ways to develop the middle of the talk, the body of the outline or the heart of the story. Finally, we presented methods for constructing conclusions.

Now it really becomes fun! Let's talk about moving your teaching beyond the predictable, through the use of *imagination.*

5

I M A G I N A T I O N

MOVE TEACHING
BEYOND THE PREDICTABLE

Several years ago Bette Midler recorded a popular song on the sound track for the movie Beaches: "You Are the Wind Beneath My Wings." It hit the charts in a big way. It is about one person supporting another: your effect on me is like the air that keeps a bird flying in the sky. The song is a thank-you sent to "my hero" for the uplifting help given to "me" on life's journey.

This musical lyric is *truth expressed in imaginary terms.* "You" are not really air; "I" am not really a bird. Instead, this song gives us a powerful metaphor, an excellent example of the power of imagination.

How comforting it is to receive God's help in the same way. He tells the children of Israel,

Do not fear, for I am with you,
  do not be afraid, for I am your God;
I will strengthen you, I will help you,
  I will uphold you with my victorious right hand.

(Isa. 41:10)

God is offering his support with a right hand. All who hear that truth or read it are expected to imagine that God is actually carrying them along. God has drawn that pic-

ture. But ask yourself this question: Where does that picture appear? It appears when you reproduce the picture
God drew in the theater of your own mind!

Here's another question: Where does the benefit come
from? You see the picture in your own mind. Then your
own production company produces the appropriate
actions in your life. "God is holding me—I do not need to
be afraid!" A picture for the nation of Israel is now trans-
posed onto your own individual screen.

All of that visualizing is available to anyone, but it
comes only by using your imagination. Each of us must
produce the picture that God has offered. If we give only
casual attention to the Lord's pictures, we may miss God's
intent.

When Jesus wanted Nicodemus to analyze the spiritual birth he was describing, he gave him a picture:

> The wind blows where it chooses, and you hear the
> sound of it, but you do not know where it comes
> from or where it goes. So it is with everyone who is
> born of the Spirit. (John 3:8)

God used pictures to communicate more effectively.
Hence, it is reasonable to assume that we should do the
same thing in our presentations at Christian meetings.

Our goal, then, is to bring about a remarkable transformation: first for ourselves in preparation, and then for
the audience. Imagination is all about *transforming ears
into eyes*. As the teacher produces pictures to be transferred to others, creative imagination is at work. Let's
break down imagination into a couple of components.

THEATER OF THE MIND: GETTING PICTURES READY FOR PROJECTION

Search for Details

The Walt Disney Company has the right idea. They call their creators *Imagineers*. They are people who create something visual out of what was visible only in someone's mind. From an individual's theater-of-the-mind, they have created a world of imagination and fantasy. Therefore, every time one of us visits Disney World or Disneyland, we fulfill that circle of imagination.

If Disney can do it, why can't we? Can we not be *imagineers* for our Christian audiences? We certainly can! From our personal picture gallery in our minds, we can create mental pictures translated into word pictures that are projected onto mind-theater-screens throughout the audience. Transmission of a clear picture is necessary for the receiver to have any guarantee of understanding what was sent.

It's important to emphasize that even the best transmission of a picture requires a quality receiver. The sender cannot do anything about the receiver, other than making the picture as clear as possible.

Here's a cartoon I observed recently, depicting how one picture was ruined:

PEOPLE WERE WAITING TO BUY TICKETS FOR THE MOVIE "TITANIC." TWO SENIORS WERE IN THE LINE TALKING ABOUT THE FAMOUS SHIP SINKING. TWO YOUNGSTERS OVERHEARD AND REMARKED, "OH, THE SHIP SINKS! THANKS FOR SPOILING THE PICTURE FOR US!"

If imagination forms pictures for mind-theaters, how can that be done? We search for details, that's how. Remember our study of Peter's visit to Simon the tanner?

Details will provide a clearer, more memorable picture.
Was there a fence around Simon the tanner's house?

Imagination provides mental pictures that are not
available to the senses—like the right hand of God, or the
wind in the sails for Nicodemus (see below). As Acts
10:17 says, there was a fence around Simon's house:

> The men sent by Cornelius found out where Simon's
> house was and stopped at the *gate*.

In answering "Was there a fence?" this verse is helpful.
If there was a gate, there must have been a fence. Ask yourself how they found Simon's house. Can you see them asking for directions? It might not seem important, but the
principle we are developing is a valid one. When you are
looking for details, project pictures in your mind; details
and pictures go together. The habit of developing details is
critical to cultivating imagination and forming pictures.

Put another way, if developing details becomes a part
of your preparation process, then you will find the details.
They will appear in places you never thought of before.
Searching for the details will become a habit.

Consider a question from another text: Did Jacob
have a memorable funeral?

This is a wonderful example of the detailing found
within the Bible itself. Jacob has just finished dividing the
land and giving instructions to his sons. Then

> he drew up his feet into the bed, breathed his last,
> and was gathered to his people. (Gen. 49:33)

If you are looking for details, nothing will escape your
eye if you pause to reflect. Even when you are reading to
an assembly, you need to see Jacob drawing up his feet,

and also drawing in his last breath. The passage notes that they took "forty days . . . for embalming" him, and that "the Egyptians wept for him seventy days" (Gen. 50:3). Those two statements form an interesting view of the times. Allow your mind to create pictures based on them.

Then Joseph received permission to take Jacob back to his homeland. All the dignitaries of Egypt went along, with horsemen and chariots. God pays attention to the details (Gen. 50:9).

Out of such information, you can develop pictures for projection. After a search of this nature, it is fairly easy to conclude that Jacob had a memorable funeral.

Simon's gate and Jacob's funeral are but two examples of ways to make the Bible come alive. Our regular practice of looking at details can move us out of the "can't listen to" and the "can listen to" categories and make us into speakers "you can't help but listen to."

See Two Things at the Same Time

Imagination and humor are much alike in that both have the ability to see two things at once. If you see a banana peel on the sidewalk, you also have the ability to see someone falling.

Jesus told Nicodemus that the Spirit is like the wind; you cannot see either. What then do you see? If your imagination is working, you can see a boat with full sails being carried along by the wind. You might not see a three-masted, square-rigged clipper ship, but some kind of sailboat will appear.

As the wind is free to move the boat, so the Spirit is free to move a person. But the sails must be up for the boat; the mind must be made ready to catch the Spirit. Just as "God is in the details" of life, so God is also in the details of imagination. Your own theater must find the details, film them, and show them on your own mind-screen.

As you create the pictures, write them down. Sketch them out, so the images are available to you for development in your teaching. From that source will come the color necessary in your delivery. If *you yourself* do not see what you are saying in your preparation, neither will your hearers see it in your delivery.

Here's another example of seeing two things at once:

God shook the earth when he gave the Ten Commandments. "The whole mountain shook violently." (Exod. 19:18)

God is going to shake the earth again, along with the heavens. "Once more I will shake not only the earth but also the heaven." (Heb. 12:26, from Hag. 2:6)

The teacher's screen must now show the earth shaking, something like an earthquake in San Francisco. Literally seeing the earth moving is essential to portraying God's former and future shaking. The past and future upheavals are then blended together into one. All this becomes a vivid portrayal of the urgency to be in a kingdom that cannot be shaken.

"So that what cannot be shaken may remain," says the Lord. (Heb. 12:27)

Now the shaking takes on full meaning for the hearers. This projection from the teacher's screen to the audience then can be used to encourage them not to "reject the one who is speaking" (Heb. 12:25).

Imagine what kind of kingdom cannot be shaken:

tion. In Isaiah 40:31, God uses the image of a soaring eagle to lift the sinking spirits of his people as he tells them to live with hope (cf. Exod. 19:4).

Eagles have been a symbol of power since Bible times. They are noted for their strength and their keen vision. With wingspans up to six feet, they portray an image of strength and freedom. To produce an image of hope, the eagle was the perfect example for God to display in order to transfer the truth about his strength and power through hope.

"Those who wait for the Lord shall renew their strength." Strength like that of an eagle will come to those who trust in the Lord. Hope is now seen as rising like an eagle. Instead of being an abstract concept, it now becomes a visual image in the mind. God now is the wind beneath their wings. Israel can be lifted above their immediate problems as they turn to the Lord.

So how do *we* produce images like that?

Imagination Connects People with Their Own Souls

During a recent Super Bowl, the communication company Nokia ran a commercial showing a number of visual images connecting people to different items in their lives. The caption stated, "Nokia connects people." They drew the pictures, then made their point.

> ONLY CONNECT! THAT WAS THE WHOLE OF
> HER SERMON.
> . . . LIVE IN FRAGMENTS NO LONGER.
> (EDWARD MORGAN FORSTER)

Leaders in Christian settings must also produce pictures to tap into the emotions and the will, where people make decisions to change, accept, or appropriate a given truth.

For example, imagination connects people to how

they have the furniture arranged in their minds, and what kinds of pictures are on the walls. Imagination, through the use of pictures, can show them what rearranging needs to be done and even move the will to do it.

Jonathan Edwards rearranged everyone's furniture when he preached his famous sermon, "Sinners in the Hands of an Angry God." He read his sermon by the light of a lantern that a young attendant held over the pages.

His pictures of hell were so vivid that people screamed and held onto things lest they fall into hell's flaming fires. That sort of imagery worked for Edward's day. It's up to each of us as communicators to decide if his approach would work for us—and if not, what would.

In another example from the Scriptures, the writer of the book of Hebrews urged his readers, "Pay greater attention to what we have heard." To drive the point home, he drew them a picture of creation, prophets, angels, Christ, the end of all things, and the eternal God. He told them to pay attention to the truth they know and to be careful not to "drift away from it" (Heb. 2:1-9).

Before sounding this warning, the writer produced numerous images for the mind-screens of the audience. He used a variety of mental pictures to rearrange the furniture in their minds.

The author says that God has spoken in a variety of ways, through—

- Prophets
- Teachers
- Angels
- Signs
- The Holy Spirit
- Scriptures
- Jesus Christ

Each of those ways provided plenty of images for the viewing pleasure of his audience. But each also provided the necessary encouragement toward change, determination, and resolve.

For our purposes, like the writer of Hebrews, the images preparing the mind for reality come from the *production company* at work. The writer of Hebrews did not make a frontal attack but spoke to the issue of lethargy.

A modern production image for lethargy could come from the Niagara River and the famous falls. Far upstream, the river is comparatively calm. Imagine you are there in your small boat. As you slowly drift with the gentle current, the warm sunshine puts you to sleep.

While sleeping, you are not aware of gradually stronger current, until the ever-increasing noise level brings you fully awake. By the time you discover the high speed of the river and the origin of the roaring noise, it is too late. You are about to go over the falls!

You can carefully produce and project such a picture on the image-screens of an audience. Most have either been to Niagara Falls or at least know about it. The seriousness of such a drift can be transferred then to the life of the Christian. Some of us drift through life without caring how we live. We are unaware of being carried along by the current of life instead of by the Lord.

In all this, we are doing more than looking for good illustrations. We are looking for ways to create images that will bring self-awareness and spiritual growth. A well-constructed image can get under or through the layers of our lives and connect with the condition of our soul. Imagination is at its most powerful when it can produce a reality check.

Everyone has imagination and some powers of creativity. We will develop these gifts only as we are willing to experiment. All of us need to expand our creativity.

Learn to Develop a Sense of Curiosity

Developing your own production company takes a lot of living, not necessarily years, but living with *curiosity*. Enlivening the imagination means not retreating from the world but engaging it. You cannot produce pictures for projection in a vacuum. A window on the world is necessary.

You cannot project relevant pictures without some sense of the world in which the hearers are living. It's not necessary for you to participate in the excesses of the world. But it is necessary for you to be aware of what's happening in the audience's world.

How can those worldly experiences be translated into images for projection? That's the question always in the forefront of the curious seeker/teacher's mind.

Living in this curiosity mode means that teachers are searchers and are intentional about making their imagination work. Making connection with people and their life experiences becomes almost an obsession.

NEVER MAKE A POINT WITHOUT AN ILLUSTRATION, AND NEVER MAKE AN ILLUSTRATION WITHOUT A POINT.

Without that intention, jargon will pile on jargon, and communication will fall flat. Developing one's creative capabilities offers some possibility that the presentation will be a human encounter, person to person.

Now we turn to a similar subject with a twist—images that really are visible and that engage the senses.

6

VISUAL IMAGES

TEACHING THAT COMES TO LIFE

We have just explored how enormously helpful the imagination is to the presentation of the Scriptures. We noted how creative mental images can uproot long-held truth-words embedded deeply enough to split self-talk from reality. Imagination, as we have seen, presents images to the mind, images of tangible things not available to the senses.

Now we want to look at presenting objects that are available to the senses, objects capable of conveying visible information. This includes object lessons for children and also the use of objects that can attract attention and carry truth into a new formation.

Some of the great cathedrals of Europe have facades, entrances, stained-glass windows, and statues that were embellished as object lessons for people unable to read. Angels are depicted doing various chores, biblical characters were illustrated, and many other scriptural scenes were available as visual aids. People can receive instruction as speakers refer to statues, paintings, or windows as aids to learning. Just walking through the doorways provides visual instruction.

In our culture, we generally reserve the use of objects for teaching children. But most of us adults have enough curiosity within us to give attention to an object held up for observation. Visual objects attract babies in the crib, children in Sunday school, and adults in Sunday morning worship or Bible study.

The kind of visualization needed is available to teachers who will give time and attention to the use of objects, allowing their imagination to do its work.

THE MAGNETIC PULL OF VISUALS

Several examples in the Bible demonstrate how visual God meant his Word to be. Take special notice of how throughout the Bible, God objectifies his whole plan of reclamation with objects that can be visualized.

Visual objects represent—

1. The origin of sin in the garden of Eden
2. The birth of a nation
3. God's protection
4. God favoring that nation
5. The eternal ascending line of God's kingdom
6. The final promised king on the throne
7. Making peace between peoples and with God
8. The new pure, clean garden of paradise

Follow the progression of matching objects:

1. Garden	Wrong fruit (Gen. 3)
2. Sand	Abraham's many offspring (Gen. 22:17)
3. Shield	The Lord protecting Abram (Gen. 15:1)
4. Apple	Israel, God's people (Deut. 32:10)
5. Lamp	Line of David forever (2 Kings 8:19)
6. Baby	Jesus as promised eternal king (Matt. 1)
7. Cross	Reconciles groups to God (Eph. 2)
8. Tree	New tree, new garden (Rev. 22)

God did not hold these objects before the people, yet they

were meant to be observed. The Lord exercised the imagination of his people by giving them objects to see, reminding them that he will always keep his promises.

In this section we are taking the example of God's use of visuals. The process moves from seeing the need for the imagination to create the object, to actually displaying something visible, and then transferring ideas from the visual to the mind.

This is the reverse of seeing something only in the mind and creating your own pictures. Ideas are now drawn from what is seen, and new pictures form in the minds of the audience.

Why do audiences young and old give attention to an object held before them?

Because *we all pay attention to something that moves.*

ONE SERVICEMAN SAID OF HIS EXPERIENCE, "WE WERE TOLD, 'IF IT DOESN'T MOVE, PAINT IT.'"

Anytime someone puts an object before us, it is magnetic. The eyes are drawn to it, and they will stay there while verbal references focus on it. So the object must be kept eye-and-ear-attractive, or it will lose its drawing power. The magnetic pull will be lost, at least temporarily, if something more compelling moves.

If someone walks by, or a baby is being carried out, or someone drops a book, the audience will turn their eyes and ears from even the most interesting object. Eyes and ears are extremely fickle.

Lay an object on the floor or hang something from the ceiling or pull an item out from a bag—what happens? People are drawn to the object, like metal to a magnet.

Why? Babies can't articulate an answer, and adults

may be too embarrassed to admit interest. But children will tell you, "I want to know what is there and why!"

We develop the subject of visuals in two steps: First, visuals you can see with your eyes, that can be handled, smelled, heard, and tasted. Second, objects that can't be seen, handled, smelled, heard, or tasted.

VISUALS SENSED

Speakers can influence all five senses by the use of visual aids. Let's look at some specific examples of seeing, hearing, touching, smelling, and tasting.

Sight

The average adult brain weighs just a little over three pounds. With its crinkled edges and shape, it looks roughly like a head of cauliflower. All the ridges and nodules can be observed in a head of cauliflower, and the weight is about the same as that of the brain.

There are scientists who have called the brain "the most complex machine in the universe," yet it weighs only fifty-one ounces. Each of us has one! Imagine that! Yet it is estimated that ordinarily a human being uses only about 10 percent of the available brain power.

The best place to find a model brain is in the grocery store. If I am speaking at a small meeting where everyone can see the floor, I draw the cauliflower out of a bag and lay it right there on the floor. For a larger audience, I keep holding it in my hand. I don't talk about it right away; I talk around it, allowing their imaginations to work. I want them to ask questions from curiosity.

The use of this "brain" can go in many directions. One possibility is showing the brain as a "decision-making house." God talks about people being alienated from him in their minds.

Once you were alienated from God and were enemies in your minds because of your evil behavior.
(Col. 1:21, NIV)

Now I can introduce the cauliflower as a model brain.
I draw their attention to the object and lay emphasis on
the mind being the place where people make the decision
to alienate themselves from God. I continually make reference to the "brain" by pointing to it on the floor or lifting it up. I make reference to it as the "house" where we
live. That keeps the image alive. It constantly reminds listeners that they also can be alienated from God by the
decisions they make.

At weddings, I have used Play Dough, taking two colors that I mold together into a ball while I am talking
about how the couple's lives blend together in marriage.
Then I mix in a third and last color, to represent the presence of God. With the three colors, the ball then becomes
multicolored and impossible to separate, as far as the
image is concerned.

Later I give them the ball as a reminder of the wedding. One couple bought a special box in which to place
the molded clay as a way of recalling the ceremony.

Sometimes I use scissors to represent two individual
lives coming together in a wedding. Holding the blades of
the scissors apart represents their individuality, and closing them signifies their binding together. I then wrap my
hand around the closed scissors to demonstrate God holding their marriage together.

For a prayer retreat or a lesson or a sermon, you can
illustrate prayer as a rope to pull us up rather than one to
pull God down. Tangle the rope with just the top emerging, thus representing God in the midst of our problems.
Then pull the rope up, allowing your hand to rise also.

The image you create is of God pulling us up.

This is a good visual and allows for the people to respond with their own ideas about prayer. It is interesting how many responses it evokes.

> **ONE LOOK IS WORTH A THOUSAND WORDS.**
> **(FRED R. BARNARD, 1921)**

Sound

The sound that I present in two parts fits a worship service, perhaps on Good Friday. I talk about the crucifixion of Jesus, leading up to the actual hanging of Jesus on the cross. The description is in the words read and spoken. So the first piece of the object lesson is made by the people hearing the words.

I have someone prepared to begin a pounding sound at the appropriate time. A heavy, solid piece of wood, some ten-penny nails, and a heavy hammer will create the sound image. Nails, wood, and hammer have to be substantial enough to make a deep sound.

Then someone drives the nails into the wood in a deliberate and measured manner, so the impact of the sounds will reflect the words just spoken. The pounding should be out of sight and unexpected. You can be assured, despite whatever shock there might be, that people will create a visual image out of sound.

Enough blows need to occur to heighten the impact and give sufficient time to understand what is taking place. The sound of the nails being struck has a moving effect on an audience. I can testify to its effectiveness.

Taste

Our Lord calls us to imagine how good he is to his people. He also wants us to imagine the land they will inherit. These all call the imagination into action:

A land flowing with milk and honey . . . (Exod. 3: 8)

O taste and see that the Lord is good;
happy are those who take refuge in him. (Ps. 34:8)

Television commercials are always challenging our taste buds with chocolate pouring over peanuts, honey flowing down on cereal, or steak cooking over an open grill. But can we produce a visual that will draw us to taste the Lord or his Word?

How sweet are your words to my taste,
sweeter than honey to my mouth!
Through your precepts I get understanding;
therefore I hate every false way. (Ps. 119:103-4)

God gave Ezekiel something to eat before sending him to speak to Israel about their wrongdoing. The Lord said,

"Son of man, eat this scroll I am giving you and fill your stomach with it." So [Ezekiel] ate it, and it tasted sweet as honey in [his] mouth." (Ezek. 3:3, NIV)

Here is one way to evoke the sense of taste with a visual. Get a piece of pita bread, a tortilla, or some kind of biscuit dough. Have the dough rolled like a scroll, or keep it flat and hold it before the audience.

Talk about the Scriptures written on scrolls, and describe a scroll. Then, after the description, eat the bread! Put honey on the bread so that when you eat it, your taste buds will show the taste throughout your expression to the audience. To conclude, you can compare the sweetness of the taste to what God promises about relating to him and his Word.

In this visual, a speaker can draw out senses of taste and sight; people see the scroll as it is being eaten. The taste is experienced not just for the person eating, but for those watching as well.

Touch

When the disciples were not sure of the identity of the risen Lord Jesus, he said:

> Look at my hands and feet; see that it is I myself.
> Touch me and see; for a ghost does not have flesh
> and bones as you see I have. (Luke 24:39)

At times crowds followed Jesus, and all who touched him were healed (Matt. 14:36; Luke 6:19). On one such occasion, a woman came up behind Jesus and "touched the fringe of his cloak." She told herself, "If I only touch his cloak, I will be made well." Jesus turned around, saw her, and declared that she was healed (Matt. 9:20-22).

Illustrating the sense of touch can be done by holding up a piece of cloth and describing Jesus wearing an outer garment. It is easy to depict the approach of the woman, her conviction that touching Jesus would heal her, and then the actual touch. He felt the touch and then turned around.

All of this scene can be developed around the idea of what it is like to touch Jesus.

Smell

Someone once experimented with a bottle of colored water with a strong aroma. He poured some of it out into a bowl before the audience, letting it flow some distance through the air. In a moment or two, he asked whether the aroma was beginning to fill the room. Soon hands went up, acknowledging the aroma all the way to the back row.

Jesus had an experience with perfume that was real and quite expensive. At Bethany, Mary took a pint of costly perfume, poured it over the feet of Jesus, and wiped his feet with her hair. Scripture says,

> The house was filled with the fragrance of the perfume. (John 12:3)

In Ephesians 5:2, Jesus himself is called "a fragrant offering and sacrifice to God" on our behalf. When Paul receives gifts from the Philippians, he calls them "a fragrant offering, a sacrifice acceptable and pleasing to God" (Phil. 4:18). Paul also says that believers are "the aroma of Christ" (2 Cor. 2:14-16; see below).

All of these examples have the possibility of bringing out the sense of smell from the Scriptures themselves. This does not mean that we have to examine and draw out every feeling. But we should be sensitive to the occurrences of the five senses in the Word.

The simplest visual for the sense of smell is to hold up a bottle of perfume, pour some out, and describe the aroma. Look for expressive words in the dictionary to stimulate the sense of smell. Then develop ideas around the washing of Jesus' feet with such expensive perfume.

Another possibility for a visual could be gifts we give to people as the Philippians gave to Paul. Some kind of wrapped box could demonstrate all kinds of giving. Then it is up to you to communicate with the right words how they are "fragrant."

Someone suggested dabbing a bit of pretend Christ perfume on the audience so that they can be the aroma of

Christ "in every place" (2 Cor. 2:14-15). You can compare this with Christians being the light of the world or the salt of the earth (Matt. 5:13-16).

I hope these few examples will encourage you to create your own visuals. Isn't it amazing that we all have that God-given fifty-one-ounce most complex machine in the universe, to use for creating, teaching, and preaching? It's just as amazing that we tap only into 10 percent of our brainpower. If we develop our creative power of imagination, we can become speakers to whom audiences can't help but listen!

VISUALS IMAGINED

These imagined visuals have the same magnetic power as the real thing, maybe more, since the audience must create the unseen image in the theater of their minds.

Sight

Here is a surefire experiment. Stop along the street and look up into the sky. People around you will do the same thing, almost by reflex. They may end up embarrassed about it, but they will look up. This is because people are curious. Presenting invisible objects might not work as well with children, but they will function effectively with young people and adults.

Many times when I speak, I describe an invisible picture on the wall. I point to it, give the details, and paint the colors in. As I point and turn my head toward the wall, the audience does the same thing. Most all of them stay with me until I have completed the picture.

It's important to remember that I never use an illustration just for the sake of using it. There is always a relationship back to the subject on which I am speaking.

I often tell an audience that I am going to write an idea

on a chalkboard. I slide or pull an invisible chalkboard out before them. I begin to spell aloud and write slowly at the same time. I even make mistakes in spelling and erase words. I keep turning to ask them if I am writing large enough, or if they can hear me when my back is turned.

Then I develop my idea, at times reviewing the material on the invisible chalkboard. This is an excellent way to keep an audience's attention. I guarantee that they will see the invisible chalkboard and the words.

You can use anything invisible if you describe it well. I have held up an imaginary world globe, given it a spin, stopped it at a certain position, and pointed to a place on the globe where the audience had missionaries. I gave it another spin and pointed to another place. People actually saw a world globe spinning—more important, they saw their missionaries around the world. Everything you do descriptively, even invisibly, is an interest-holder for your main thoughts.

Touch

Suppose you want to develop the scene of Jesus touching someone (as in Mark 3:10; 10:13) instead of being touched, as the woman touched him (see above). The idea of Bill Gaither's song "He Touched Me" can be expanded with invisible objectivity.

Ask each person in the audience to imagine walking along a busy road. It will help if you ask them to close their eyes. You want each of them to get away from the noise, traffic, and problems. Tell them to visualize a path that leads into a woods. As you walk, you notice someone coming toward you. The two of you come closer, and you see someone who looks like Jesus to you.

As you meet, the man even identifies himself as Jesus. You are overcome by the encounter. He talks, and you are comforted, even feeling a sense of relief from your burdens. Satisfied that you have a true encounter with Jesus, you are not frightened, but overjoyed when he puts his arm around your shoulder. After further brief conversation, Jesus disappears. Your entire being is afire, and you say aloud, *"He touched me!"*

For a moment you remain at the site of the adventure, then you turn back on the path that leads to the busy road. But things are different now. You say it again: *"He touched me!"*

Smell

Paul says that Christians have a special aroma,

> the fragrance that comes from knowing [Christ]. For we are the aroma of Christ to God among those who are being saved and among those who are perishing; to the one a fragrance from death to death, to the other a fragrance from life to life (2 Cor. 2:14-16).

Possibilities abound with this illustration of the Christian role in life. One is that Christians have the smell of death to nonbelievers, who only see self-sacrifice. Christian fragrance becomes a conscience for unbelievers.

You can describe rescue workers wearing masks while taking dead bodies from the aftermath of an earthquake or flood. The stench of death and disease is so offensive that it must be avoided.

On the other hand, you may describe walking into a greenhouse filled with spring and summer flowers prepared for planting. It's like the sweet fragrance of one Christian to another or to those searching for life. "Through us spreads *in every place* the fragrance" of knowing Christ (2 Cor. 2:14). You can ask, "What kind of aroma do you exude *in every place?*"

Sound

Can an audience hear a sound that is not audible? Can the imagination produce such a sensation?

> **IF A TREE FALLS WHEN NO ONE IS AROUND, DOES IT MAKE A SOUND?**

Jesus told Nicodemus that he could hear the sound of the wind but could not see it. Nicodemus certainly had an idea of that sound as he listened to Jesus.

Ponder this verse:

In a moment, in the twinkling of an eye, at the last trumpet. For the trumpet will sound, and the dead will be raised imperishable, and we will be changed.
(1 Cor. 15:52)

You could say or sing a portion of the hymn "When the trumpet of the Lord shall sound and time shall be no more. . . ." Or you may hold up an imaginary trumpet and blow it to make sounds as for introducing a VIP or summoning the people (e.g., Isa. 27:13; Joel 2:15). Then pause and ask the audience if they can hear the last trumpet making its call. Give them time for reflection.

Taste

A young man serving the remaining years of his eight-year prison sentence was dramatically changed into a Christian person. During that change, he was introduced to the Bible. He said he could not get enough of it and remarked, "I took it in great gulps." He meant that he read large sections at a time. But I could literally see him eating the Word for the first time. It tasted so good to him that he just kept on eating (cf. Jer. 15:16; Rev. 10:8-11).

In a dramatic action, you can hold the Bible in front of you; then without saying anything, move your head as if you are reading a lot of Scripture and enjoying it. Turn several pages to give the impression of tasting a large amount of it. Take it in big gulps. It would be like eating a butter-soaked ear of corn; pause, add "with pleasure," and smile.

Like Peter says, "Long for the pure, spiritual milk, so that by it you may grow into salvation—if indeed you have tasted that the Lord is good" (1 Pet. 2: 3).

Draw out the taste buds. Just say to the audience, "A cold glass of milk and Oreo cookies." Pause. Let the taste-image form. However you do it, make the image-suggestion deliberate. Then give them time to allow the picture to develop.

Anyone who speaks in Christian settings knows how important it is to hold the attention of a gathering of people. So when there is such an attention-getter like a visual display, follow God's lead and make things visual.

The Bible does it best:

> We declare to you what was from the beginning, what we have *heard*, what we have *seen* with our eyes, what we have *looked at* and *touched* with our hands, concerning the word of life. (1 John 1:1, emphasis added)

John uses three of the five senses to prove the life of Jesus. The illustration points out what we all need to learn: the more senses we evoke, the more likely we are to have audiences listen to us. So use that fifty-one-ounce most complex machine in the universe and develop your creativity!

Now we move to the subject of humor, which someone has called "a serious communication tool." Let's see how humor can spice up our teaching.

7

Humor

A Valuable Spice to Your Teaching

Norman Cousins, former editor of the *Saturday Review*, raised question marks for the medical profession. In the mid-1960s, while battling a severe connective tissue disease, he checked himself out of his hospital room. With the aid of a sympathetic doctor, he experimented with different medications and added regular doses of humor.

Cousins discovered that watching funny movies and laughing could give him several hours of painless sleep. From those experiences with humor, his writings inspired the medical profession to take serious interest in humor.

He has taught the benefits of humor at a medical school! Cousins calls humor "train wrecks of the mind," because a joke or a funny story will take us down one path and end up on another.

For the Christian communicator, humor and laughter are valuable in presenting gospel truth. Since the Bible itself offers opportunity for laughter, it sets a healthy precedent for us to follow. We want to look at being funny *on purpose*—humor has to be in the right places.

Humor and Its Companion, Laughter

In the teaching process, one cannot overestimate the

value of humor to attract listeners:
- Humor is to teaching what salt is to a T-bone steak and potatoes. Both make things taste better.
- Humor is to teaching what oil is to gears. They both make things run smoother.
- Humor can produce laughter, and those smiles of joy are releasing tension. Using humor in teaching makes listening possible and learning probable. Most people like to laugh, smile, or at least feel that inner tickle.
- Humor shakes salt and pepper into the teaching situation by making people want to hear. When listeners pay attention, they learn more. The business world, the medical profession, therapists, and most other vocations have accepted humor as standard procedure. Therefore, those who teach the Scriptures in any setting must consider humor as a serious tool for communication.
- Humor is the ability to see two things at once. You see one event and picture another with its funny side up. A humorous story leads you one direction and ends up in another, bringing out smiles or laughter. The unexpected turn makes you laugh, as in this medical humor:

ARTERY: THE STUDY OF PAINTINGS.
DILATE: TO LIVE A LONG TIME.

Even the government can be funny:

THE LORD'S PRAYER: 66 WORDS.
LINCOLN'S GETTYSBURG ADDRESS:
286 WORDS.
THE DECLARATION OF INDEPENDENCE:
1,322 WORDS.
REGULATIONS ON SELLING CABBAGE:
26,911 WORDS.

No wonder a recent business journal noted, "Humor is a serious communication tool." In various professions, humor is valuable because it does indeed make communication smoother in a nonthreatening way. Through its use, people are opened up to learning.

While listeners like laughter, not every Christian teacher uses humor as a regular spice. But we can and should acquire humor and practice using it.

TOURIST: HOW DO I GET TO CARNEGIE HALL?
CABBIE: PRACTICE!

Since Norman Cousins' groundbreaking work with humor, many studies have shown that laughter can raise oxygen levels and help the condition of the heart.

Humor generally comes in one of three packages:

• The target is yourself.
• The target is someone else.
• The target is a situation.

Directing humor at yourself is the least risky and the most effective. If the target is another individual, you need to exercise great care. Targeting a situation falls somewhere between the two and is reasonably safe.

Some people can be funny in some circumstances, but not in front of an audience. One may fear not being funny when wanting to be so; that tends to stifle a person. It can even affect someone as professional as Jay Leno.

Leno works long hours and claims to sleep only four hours a night. His fear is not being fully funny. With his writers, he works his material over and over, so that he can be as confident as possible that he will draw laughs.

For those who are not spontaneously funny, it is a good idea to plan spots of humor ahead of time. That way, you don't have to worry about omitting humor. The risk is that the humor may sound contrived or be out of place. You can remedy that by using humor with relevance to the immediate theme.

Someone described humor as "an expected future replaced with an unexpected future. The more unexpected, the better."

WHAT DAY OF THE YEAR IS A COMMAND?
MARCH FOURTH.

Surprise opens up pathways to the mind that otherwise may be blocked. It takes skill to get through hardened layers of old opinions. Hearers are less likely to see the need for change if speakers simply try to beat truths into their heads. Humor can be the assistant, drawing pictures, opening closed doors, catching people unawares, and helping them stay with the teacher. People enjoy hearing something funny. They are likely to remember it and associate it with something serious.

Humor brings results that are defined by the listeners. It may be a smile or a laugh.

A YOUNG BOY PLAYING BASEBALL WAS VERY
ENCOURAGED, EVEN THOUGH HIS TEAM WAS
LOSING FOURTEEN TO NOTHING. WHEN ASKED
HOW HE COULD BE SO UPBEAT, HE REPLIED,
"WE HAVEN'T BEEN UP TO BAT YET!"

THE BIBLE AND HUMOR

The Word of God is not without humor. In fact, the Scripture says that the Lord laughs at the wicked rulers of the earth (Ps. 2:4). Connecting laughter with God is an intriguing thought.

The Teacher says laughter should be a part of life:

For everything there is a season,
  and a time for every matter under heaven: . . .
  a time to weep, and a time to laugh. (Eccles. 3:1, 4)

A heart that has some laughter in it has taken good medicine, Solomon says in Proverbs 17:22:

A cheerful heart is a good medicine,
  but a downcast spirit dries up the bones.

Little wonder that all professions are including laughter in the workplace. Laughter is also the spice of teaching, so it belongs in the learning place as well.

In my own speaking, I often draw humor and laughter from a passage in the New Testament. The Scripture says, "Do not let the sun go down on your anger" (Eph. 4:26).

I explain the importance of settling disagreements before bedtime, so a problem does not fester overnight and give Satan "a foothold" (Eph. 4:25, NIV).

After I explain the principle, I tell my audience that my wife and I have always settled our differences before we went to bed. Then I pause and add, *"One year we were up for three months!"*

That comment rings true: first, the audience has experienced what every family has—disagreements. Second, the unexpected and exaggerated ending puts power into it. That's why it's called a punch line. It's supposed to get a laugh.

So at that moment, all in the audience are doing the same thing. They are laughing and remembering pieces of their own family struggles. After the humor, the speaker can develop the serious matter of settling disagreements. The group will have listening ears.

Something of the outrageous made Abraham laugh. The Lord told him that he and Sarah would have a son. It seemed so far of out of range for him that "Abraham fell on his face and laughed" (Gen. 17:17). After all, he was one hundred years old, and Sarah was ninety.

> **WHEN THIS 100-YEAR-OLD FELL ON HIS FACE, WHO HELPED HIM UP?**

Sarah laughed when she heard the Lord promise them a child. When the Lord asked about the laughter, she was afraid and lied: "I did not laugh" (Gen. 18:12-15). But when Isaac was born, she said, "God has brought laughter for me; everyone who hears will laugh with me" (Gen. 21:6). Sarah's laughter is the expression of joy, the smile of satisfaction.

Like the softness of God's touch on a soul racked by grief, so the wise teacher will refer to a Scripture that touches a tender spot. A smile will emerge, a nod hardly noticeable may happen—a touch of joy.

Nehemiah told the people to stop grieving and encouraged them: "The joy of the Lord is your strength" (Neh. 8:10b). He wanted them to laugh inside and feel good about God. Christian communicators have such a wonderful opportunity to bring joy and laughter to people. The Scriptures offer many occasions to provide a smile, a touch of joy, a burst of laughter.

BEING FUNNY ON PURPOSE

To be fully appreciated, does humor require an audience? I think not. If the teacher can enjoy a good funny story alone, or if one can laugh at oneself, that is a wonderful way to loosen the grip of fear. In other words, humor *does* require an audience, though it may be as small as an audience of one.

Being able to laugh at yourself is a sure sign of self-assurance. If you can think funny, you can learn.

Think about Ziggy feeling depressed and unwanted. He is sitting on the psychiatrist's couch, in need of consoling. The counselor assures him,

THE WHOLE WORLD ISN'T AGAINST YOU. BILLIONS OF PEOPLE DON'T CARE ONE WAY OR THE OTHER.

To produce laughter on purpose, surround yourself with items that make you laugh! A good teacher is always preparing to maintain a level of humor and then finding material spiced with the laughter of life.

Think about these questions: How many times do the children laugh with you in a class? How many times do the adults laugh? Do they laugh with you or at you? Do you search out what makes you laugh? How often?

How does one find humor on purpose? You need to learn to see the funny side of life; all you have to do is look for it. Venture out and find humor anywhere:

- Read bumper stickers.
- Read T-shirts.
- Go to an airport and just watch the people.
- Read billboards.
- Observe people driving in rush-hour traffic.
- Read the newspaper ads.
- Read joke books.
- Observe parents and children at the mall.
- Read human-interest stories in magazines.

As a general rule, material that is original or adapted by the speaker works best. If you have made it your own, you feel more comfortable with it. You will be more natural and effective from putting some of your own creativity into the humor.

I like to use unexpected paradox in my speaking.

> **FRANK BORROWS SAMMY'S CAR. LATER FRANK CALLS TO TELL HIS FRIEND THAT HE IS HAVING CAR TROUBLE.**
> **SAMMY ASKS "WHAT'S WRONG WITH IT?"**
> **"WATER IN THE CARBURETOR," HIS FRIEND REPLIES.**
> **"ALL RIGHT, I'LL CHECK IT. WHERE'S THE CAR?"**
> **"IN THE RIVER," FRANK RESPONDS.**

I would not hesitate to use this joke to demonstrate the paradox of the gospel. Just as you expect water in the carburetor to mean just that and not have "river" as the answer, so the cross is equally as paradoxical. You would never expect life to come from a dead body.

I say to my audience, "Isn't it strange and unexpected to hear 'river' as the location of the car?" Then I add, "Isn't it strange and unexpected to hear the gospel saying the *cross* is how our separation from God is taken away?"

As a communicator, do whatever it takes to get spice for your Truth-telling. People must listen and be helped to act. Humor is a valuable tool to help transfer the Truth.

By now I am sure you are convinced how important humor is to your presentation. Yet being funny at the wrong time is always possible, so let's look at some ways to guard our humor.

HUMOR IN ALL THE RIGHT PLACES

If we use humor in the right way, it can be just what the doctor ordered to keep our audience's attention. We certainly don't want anyone drifting off to sleep.

> A LIGHTHOUSE KEEPER WAS ACCUSTOMED TO THE FOGHORN SOUND AT MIDNIGHT EVERY MIDNIGHT. ONE NIGHT IT DIDN'T SOUND. HE WOKE UP AND SAID, "WHAT'S THAT?"

A teacher should not avoid humor, but we need to address inappropriate humor. Here are some guidelines to keep your use of humor on track:

- Avoid put-down humor.
- Ask yourself, "Is anyone likely to get hurt by using this joke or story?"
- Be aware that spontaneous humor risks offending someone.
- Is the humor relevant to the situation?
- Can I deliver the story confidently?
- Have I practiced enough to be comfortable?
- Does this humor show respect for the people involved?

Some say you should not laugh at your own jokes or stories; let the audience decide whether or not they are funny. Though I understand that the audience makes the final decision, I also must confess that if I am telling a story that amuses me, I often smile or laugh at its conclusion. I hasten to add that I never fake a laugh for laughter's sake.

Humor can transform you, my friend.

> **TWO CATERPILLARS WERE TALKING AND NOTICED A BUTTERFLY FLYING OVER THEM. THE ONE CATERPILLAR SAID TO THE OTHER, "YOU'LL NEVER GET ME UP IN ONE OF THOSE THINGS!"**

If the crowd doesn't think my joke is funny, I follow it up with a comment that will keep the humor alive. I am not embarrassed if the joke bombs. The key is to allow humor to make its home in your heart. If it comes naturally, fine. If it doesn't, then invite it into your life. It is the spice that will keep your teaching alive.

Since God put humor in the Bible, we ought to use the Bible to put humor into people's lives.

PART THREE

WHAT DO I NEED TO KNOW ABOUT DELIVERY?

8

Being Yourself

The Key to Effective Delivery

Some wise man said that the only time we are honestly being ourselves is when we are all alone. Most other times we are putting on a show for someone else. There's a sharp edge to that statement, yet a measure of truth within it. We do put on many faces, so being yourself is no easy matter—especially in delivering the Scriptures.

The Bible does point to the serious nature of being yourself and also how to make that happen:

> The purposes in the human mind are like deep water, but the intelligent will draw them out. (Prov. 20:5)

> Give me an undivided heart to revere your name.
> (Ps. 86:11)

> For out of the abundance of the heart the mouth speaks. (Matt. 12:34)

> The good person out of the good treasure of the heart produces good. (Luke 6:45)

The key to effective delivery is found in these scriptural guidelines. Reverence for the Lord overflows a full heart. Such a speaker is transparent and understanding, with a focus on the Lord that becomes the driving force in their presentation.

Since the very purpose of your presence before an audience is to speak or teach from the Scripture, you must deliver the Truth from deep within. You reveal your very being. Indeed, it is the Truth by which you live.

As you expose your heart, you earnestly let the audience see and feel what you are seeing and feeling. When a person is being moved by feelings, the real self emerges. The purposes that are deep within will flow with understanding, and the audience will know that what you are delivering is worth their attention.

Being yourself is not like the newspaper boy throwing the paper at the door. That act is cold, with no personal communication. Instead, think of yourself as a florist delivering roses to the door. Through that act, you communicate feeling.

In piano contests, amateurs play the same piece of music. Someone wins, the rest don't. Yet they all touch the same keys, observe the same timing, play the same notes. The winner has done more, revealing something of the real self in presenting the piece.

This is also true about teachers. They may all use the same words, but if something of the inner self emerges, the audience is compelled to listen. A philosophy professor once said, *"We are alike because we are all different."* We don't all touch words the same way.

> A CHILD ONCE SAID, "BECAUSE OF GEORGE WASHINGTON, I ONCE TOLD THE TRUTH EVEN THOUGH I THOUGHT I MIGHT GET IN TROUBLE. I WAS RIGHT."

It is this difference in approach that we need to explore for Christian communicators. The difference is not in the material. Two people can take the same text and deliver a message. One plunges through deep waters, delivering with understanding and a sense of urgency. The second person speaks in mediocre terms.

The audience ultimately senses whether or not you are being yourself. But the defining moment for you is whether you have a sense of communication from deep within. You need to be able to say from your soul, "I am here to help you believe."

The meaning for being yourself comes out of experience and a solid sense of what is "really real." We stand under the authority of that reality, earnestly desiring to help people believe Christian truth. When we do that, we are truly ourselves.

LIVING WATER FROM THE WELL WITHIN

Being yourself starts with your relationship with Christ. Persons who believe the Scriptures, trust in the Savior, and are daily led by the Spirit—they are the ones Jesus describes in the Gospel of John:

> Out of the believer's heart shall flow rivers of living water. (John 7:38)

Christian communicators must always draw from that deep wellspring. They have to dig the well personally, motivated by their own yearning to be alive with the living God.

To fully be yourself is to know you are being influenced and touched by God's Spirit every day. Down deep there is a strong pillar of belief that sustains you and invisibly supports your presentation of the Truth.

This is evident in Paul's writings:

> For this reason I suffer as I do. But I am not
> ashamed, for I know the one in whom I have put my
> trust, and I am sure that he is able to guard until
> that day what I have entrusted to him. (2 Tim. 1:12)

The apostle was drawing from a deep source. When
he was being himself, the water was always the water of
life—Jesus. He was not ashamed. He was always trying to
persuade people. Paul wanted to do whatever he could to
help them believe.

Being yourself in front of listeners certainly requires at
least some measure of the depth expressed by Paul.
Confidence about being yourself is directly related to
what you are all about, deep down inside. A shallow well
will not provide confidence.

**GIVE THE WORLD THE BEST YOU HAVE,
AND IT MAY NEVER BE ENOUGH;
GIVE THE WORLD THE BEST YOU'VE GOT
ANYWAY.
(MOTHER TERESA)**

Peter reveals his own depth of soul when he remem-
bers the acts of Jesus. He reflects on his days with the
Lord:

> God anointed Jesus of Nazareth with the Holy Spirit
> and with power; . . . he went around doing good and
> healing all who were oppressed by the devil, for God
> was with him. We are witnesses to all that he did.
> (Acts 10:38-39)

Putting the right touch on words will make us witnesses who can also release people through the persuasion of our personal being. This is more than mere words—what the words mean to the speaker will become evident. Paul sets the standard for personal being:

Be imitators of me, as I am of Christ. (1 Cor. 11:1)

If the effort in preaching or teaching is not preceded by following the example of Christ, then being yourself will be too much like yourself! Someone can be a good teacher and yet not be the self that God desires.

Paul never gave up on that standard of following Jesus and counting Jesus as his example. He was relentless in his quest to be a banner for Truth. He always made plain who he was; his passion must have been obvious.

Nevertheless, we need some caution. Intensity alone is not the answer to being yourself. While passionate delivery may exhibit one's style, it does not necessarily demonstrate depth. The person with a great amount of intensity may only produce easily dissolved cotton candy, whereas someone else may give birth to persuasion.

Therefore, what counts is not merely who you are, but rather who you are inside and whether it shows the depth of knowing God.

This means knowing who we are and knowing the person we most want to be like. We must constantly go to the source of our identity. So how do we become these streams of living water that flow from deep within?

LIVING WATER FROM AN INVENTIVE MIND

An inventive mind is a personal creation born from desire and thought. Here is a question worth considering: *How can I be a florist and not a paper boy?* We need to deliver ideas with a personal touch, not just throw them on the porch. As we give thought to new forms, we change a stagnant pool into a stream.

Inventing new vocabulary is a good place to start. Don't throw away the old words, but breathe new life into your speech with words that have been upgraded. There are many words you can add to the old ones, making them brighter.

For example, instead of saying *salvation*, how about one of these synonyms?

- deliverance
- surviving
- protection
- lifeline
- rescue
- reclamation

WHEN A COWBOY ROUNDS UP HORSES, HE PUTS THEM IN A CHORALE.

Using new words will help you invent new sentences, new ideas, and new illustrations. Every new word offers a new picture for you. As an example, take the word *lifeline* and place it on your mental screen. What images appear from life? Place the word *salvation* in its place and see what the image suggests.

I see a photograph of a large hook hanging from a construction crane. This image came to me as I remembered and mentally placed the word *lifeline* alongside the word *salvation*. I had formed a spontaneous invention or creation. Similarly, a harness hanging from a rescue helicopter could enhance the image of salvation.

The same inventive quality is available to everyone.

One simply needs to draw from the wellspring, letting it become a stream of living water. A literal stream of water is never the same. It is ever new, ever changing. Only the source remains the same. So it is with the water that Jesus promises to us.

Perhaps we need a change in the way we bring Scriptures to our minds. Maybe we need to do a makeover of the way the Bible enters our thoughts. Hotels don't use keys anymore. They have replaced them with card-entry systems. As a Christian communicator, it's time to change our entry systems for the Bible. We need to invent new ways.

As you make your way into the Bible, see it as the source of your own personal stream of living water. The Ohio River flows into the mighty Mississippi at Cairo, Illinois. There the two become one great river. In the same way, let the Bible become one with you. In doing so, you become a potential source of belief as you allow the mighty power of God to do its transforming work.

Invent new ways to flavor your speaking. Practice changing the speed at which you deliver some words. Look at the possibility that you're saying everything at the same rate, though in your ordinary conversation, change comes naturally.

Ask yourself whether you deliver all the words in the same pitch. In your normal conversation, you raise and lower your voice for emphasis without giving it a thought. Listen to people in conversation sometime and notice how the variable speed and pitch come naturally.

Pay attention to your eyes. Where is the focus? Can you look into the eyes of people, or do you tend to gaze toward the ceiling or the back wall? If so, why is eye-to-eye contact uncomfortable for you?

If you are not able to look at your audience, you give

the impression that what you are presenting is not all that important, or that you are nervous. Television advertisers look you in the eye. The company paying the bills wouldn't have it any other way. That's direct and personal communication.

The lesson is clear: Paying strict attention to your personal mannerisms is part of being yourself.

LIVING WATER FROM A BOLD SOUL

If our fear of speaking sometimes troubles us, we ought to emulate Peter and pray for great boldness as he did in the book of Acts:

> And now, Lord, . . . grant to your servants to speak your word with all boldness. (Acts 4:29)

What makes this statement even more powerful is that Peter speaks these words after his court appearance for speaking publicly about Jesus! We can see the same boldness in Paul's life. Writing from prison, he asked the Ephesians,

> Pray also for me, so that when I speak, a message may be given to me to make known with boldness the mystery of the gospel. (Eph. 6:19)

Notice that even the deep wells within Peter and Paul needed prayer to allow boldness to bring forth living streams of water. Picture Peter just returning from court after he was arrested for telling the truth about Jesus. Think of Paul in prison's chains for the same reason.

They don't ask for mercy or pity. They don't ask for better treatment or better food. They want more fearlessness to go right back out on the street and live on the edge.

So what, you may ask, does that have to do with being yourself? Everything.

Just being deeply spiritual is not a guarantee that living water will flow from within. It will take all of the inventiveness you have, *plus* a measure of boldness from your soul.

Remember what Jesus said about the stones in Luke 19:40? If the people who shouted "Hosanna" were silenced, the stones would cry out. The truth about him must be spoken.

Boldness gives a rush to the current of the stream flowing from you like water going over rapids. It is not the speed in your delivery—instead, enthusiasm is what counts. This is not misguided religious emotion, but excitement rushing up from inside.

In fact, the word *enthusiasm* comes from roots that originally meant "god-insideness." Enthusiasm can be artificially induced, but that's not being yourself. Boldness can make the excitement genuine, a natural expression of the real you.

Be bold! Ask someone who hears your teaching to rate your level of enthusiasm. You may discover that you're not coming off in an exciting way. Perhaps you are in a teaching position that you do not desire, and the result is a less-than-enthusiastic delivery.

Whatever the situation, the Bible is still your source of information. To be a successful teacher, you must show enthusiasm that flows from personal conviction.

If you do ask someone about your speaking style and they suggest you need more boldness, what should you do? First, don't quit. Salespeople are trained to think positively and enthusiastically about their sales presentations by imagining that they are exciting people. They practice being excited about the product. What a great idea!

Thus, if you want a more exciting delivery, you need to imagine it happening, and then *practice*. Read to discover more about your product-source. Learn what it promises the buyers. Catch a glimpse of the excitement of God coming to us on earth!

Your experience in sharing Bible truth before an audience ought to be exciting. You can be enthusiastic as your bold soul is developed. Success in teaching begins with *desire*. You must really want to be an earnest and enthusiastic teacher.

LIVING WATER FROM A FREE SPIRIT

A free spirit has the self-determination to be loose about trying new approaches to teaching and speaking. We need to become unafraid to fail and be willing to experiment.

> **THEY TOLD THE YOUNG MAN IT COULDN'T BE DONE. WITH A GRIN, HE SET HIMSELF TO IT. HE TACKLED THE JOB THAT COULDN'T BE DONE, AND BEHOLD, HE COULDN'T DO IT. (PARODY OF EDGAR GUEST'S "IT COULDN'T BE DONE")**

Think about the following issues and answer honestly about your own speaking style:

- How is my posture? Do I slouch? Do I lean?
- Do I move at all?
- How can my body help me more?
- Does my face show enthusiasm?
- Do I shuffle my notes nervously?
- What could I change to allow myself more freedom in my speaking?

- Is my spirit free enough to experiment with objects for illustrating points?
- Can I smile more?
- Can my eyes be more expressive?
- Are my words sluggish or clear?
- Does my voice drop at the end of sentences?
- Does the audience keep losing my ideas?
- Who can I ask to monitor and evaluate my delivery?

Are you free enough to ask yourself all these questions? Being yourself in delivery is certainly all about inner strength that is released from a free spirit.

Yellowstone National Park has over 200 geysers that erupt on average every 30 minutes. Geothermal heat rises from deep in the earth. When underground water flows over the hot molten magma, it boils and expands. The water and steam are under tremendous pressure. Plumes of boiling water burst forth through cracks in the earth, shooting as high as sixty feet in the air.

Something like that is true of the free spirit. Plumes of Truth burst forth from the core of our being. The energy is evident to our audience. It's possible to have heat at the core of our being but no cracks at the surface to let it burst forth. A free spirit works at making those cracks.

Free spirits let the Holy Spirit carry them, always open to accepting what is offered. In describing the prophets who spoke for God, Peter says:

No prophecy ever came by human will, but men and women carried along by the Holy Spirit spoke from God. (2 Peter 1:21, NRSV/NIV)

We will never be prophets of old, but being "carried along" is certainly not beyond the experience of a modern-day free spirit. Read the rest of the first chapter of 2 Peter to see that the prophets did not serve themselves. Instead, what they received was for someone else. They weren't even aware of how far-reaching their influence would be!

In his letter to the Romans, Paul shares another interesting fact about our spirit:

> It is that very Spirit bearing witness with our spirit that we are children of God. (Rom. 8:16)

God's Spirit actually communicates with your spirit, if your spirit is free enough to accept what is being passed along. This means more than just belonging to God as his child. There is person-to-person communication.

Jesus told his disciples that they would sometimes be on trial and have to give an account for their faith:

> Do not worry beforehand about what you are to say; but say whatever is given you at that time, for it is not you who speak, but the Holy Spirit. (Mark 13:11)

How do speakers know they are being carried along by God? How does that knowledge bring you to a sense of being yourself?

Begin by asking God to carry you along as you prepare and when you deliver Truth to an audience. As you continue to ask and ask, say to yourself, "God is carrying me along."

Words will come to you, ideas will emerge, materials will appear, and articles will arrive that will meet your needs. The Holy Spirit will work with your spirit so that Jesus gets the credit.

> The Advocate, the Holy Spirit, whom the Father will
> send in my name, will teach you everything, and
> remind you of all that I have said to you. (John
> 14:26)

The Spirit does not call attention to himself, but points us
to the Lord Jesus.

A free spirit hangs loose before God's Spirit and actually expects to be carried along. The invisible Spirit joins
my spirit, forming a union of two beings intent on delivering the Truth. When your free spirit allows that union,
you are being yourself.

In the colonial town of Williamsburg, Virginia, you
are likely to see a man guiding a team of oxen, pulling a
wagon. The movement is slow, but the team stays in perfect rank with each other. Over the neck of each ox is the
bow of the yoke that holds them together. As long as they
stay side by side, the yoke is even. But if one falls behind
or pulls ahead, the yoke will bind them. It's the same for
our relationship with God's Spirit.

Being carried is a more intimate look than you at first
may have considered. But it's not an impossible position.
The prophets sensed God speaking to them in a manner
we don't understand. But can't we as Christian communicators experience God caring for us in an image of being
carried along? I think so.

It is such a wonderful image in establishing how you
present yourself naturally before a group of listeners.

In this chapter, we have seen that being yourself is
having a sense of communication. It's an earnest desire to
deliver biblical truth in the image of a florist delivering
roses, rather than a newsboy throwing papers. To find
that sense and desire to help people believe, we draw from
a deep well of personally appropriated Truth.

Regarding practical matters, there are paths that can guide us. We need an inventive mind, a bold soul, and a free spirit united in partnership with God's Spirit, who carries and holds the union together.

The next chapter looks at the most available method of delivery to guarantee maximum attentiveness from an audience—conversation.

9

Conversational Approach

A Better Way of Delivery

Conversation in preaching or teaching is the most direct highway to the mind. Yet it's often not easy and not used.

That's fascinating, isn't it? A natural communication tool such as conversation is so accessible, yet often not easy. When is it not easy?

- If you're around people you don't know.
- If you're unsure of your position.
- If your mouth is full.
- If you're with people much older or younger than you.
- If you are preaching or teaching.

But conversation *is* easy when—

- You argue and others seem to be hard of hearing, so you shout louder!
- You are among close friends.
- Your mouth is not full.
- You are comfortable with yourself in any company, including the audience.

No doubt you can list other situations where you might be comfortable or uncomfortable in conversation.

Let us regard conversation as a valuable communication tool for speaking. Here's why I believe it is so valuable:

THE CLOSER SPEAKERS CAN COME TO CONVERSATION, THE MORE SURE THEY ARE OF BEING HEARD.

Conversation should be a natural choice for speakers. For some of us, almost all our waking hours involve communicating through conversation! It has all the necessary ingredients for good preaching or teaching. But they are so natural that we never notice them. All the nonverbal body moves, the pitch, the speed, pauses, phrases—everything is at our natural discretion.

We don't think of any of these things when we talk. But in public speaking, these same ingredients don't come naturally, so we have to supply them. The audience makes the difference because we don't see ourselves as being in conversation with anyone.

Preachers and teachers run the risk of being lecture-oriented. While they may desire to communicate, being in front of an audience brings them fear, and fear hinders the freedom of the conversational approach. Furthermore, regular speaking forms deep ruts of speech habits.

When you listen to people talking, they don't speak in long sentences like the ones you just read. Phrases are generally short and to the point. Pauses supply space for reflection and thought about what comes next. Emotion brings emphasis. Usually the body responds appropriately. All you need to communicate comes naturally, when you don't have an audience.

Have you ever experienced this situation? A person is speaking loudly to overcome crowd noise. The word is passed around the room that someone is going to lead a prayer of thanks for the meal. Everyone gets quiet, except our friend, Mr. Loudmouth. He didn't hear the announcement. His embarrassment is obvious.

The discomfort comes from the sudden quietness, but it is more than that. The ingredient of having an audience has been added to the self-consciousness.

Self-consciousness has a way of allowing nervousness to arise in any setting. The limiting effect increases when we consider the means of communication to deliver a message to an audience.

Therefore, let's inquire into the art of conversation. Our investigation will center around what conversation is and how it works. Though it will be an over-simplification, it will still be helpful. Then we will apply the findings to teaching and preaching.

How Conversation Works

Conversation sends and receives information. It exchanges experiences. It offers greetings. Messages are sent nonverbally and verbally—often the nonverbal element is stronger than the verbal.

Without taking much thought, conversation comes easy. Even though conversation is a creative act, the words flow without much effort because ideas are present. We talk from our thoughts quite naturally.

> A YOUNG MAN SAID HIS GIRLFRIEND HAD AN UPPER-PLATE DENTURE. WHEN ASKED HOW HE KNEW, HE SAID IT JUST CAME OUT IN THE CONVERSATION.

Think about participating in an argument. The words can come in gusts from one to two hundred words per minute! The more intense the argument, the faster and louder the words get. It's as though both parties have suddenly become hard of hearing.

When we talk naturally, we form the sentences easily and quickly. Nervousness and fear are not present in normal social conversations. Over grocery carts, people chat casually to friends they haven't seen in a long time. No effort is needed to create dialogue.

Men leaning against the fenders of their pickup trucks have no trouble putting short-clipped sentences together. They may be recounting last night's football game or a recent fishing trip. The words come effortlessly.

They are talking about something that interests them, something they know. Maybe they're offering expert advice to the losing coach on what he should have done last night to win the game!

By the grocery cart or pickup truck, creativity takes place without any of the parties realizing it: a touch of enthusiasm here, some eye contact there, some hand movements over the large fish, some pauses now and then until thoughts catch up. No nervousness!

Imagination works smoothly to supply the necessary mental pictures for the fishing trip. The lake, the boat, the sunshine, the fish on the line—these all give energy to the fisherman telling his story. Smiles appear on the faces of the hearers. In their imaginations, they have seen it all.

Why does such conversation work? Because the fisherman, without realizing or intending it, uses his imagination to recall his fishing trip. He uses his hands to describe the size of the fish, and he reenacts the whole tale. All of it is quite natural—he gives no thought to the mechanics of conversation.

Consider this telephone conversation. It's Monday morning, and two people are talking about yesterday's sermon. Nothing visual is going on, except in the mind.

"Did you understand what he was trying to say yesterday?"

"I'm not sure I did [pause]. I tried to listen [pause], but the sermon rambled."

"Well, was there a point he was trying to make?"

"I think there was a point. I got the impression [pause] that gossip is wrong. But the word was never used."

"That's strange [pause]. I didn't get that point at all. It seemed to me that the idea of the sermon was about witnessing."

"I guess neither one of us got the point" [pause].

"I wish the pastor would just talk to us instead of [pause] preaching. Maybe we could understand more."

"Were you able to get any pictures from what he was saying?"

"None at all [pause]. I couldn't see what was being said."

"Oh, well [pause]. Say, did you hear that John and Debbie are splitting up?"

"No! [long pause]. When did this happen? Tell me more about it!"

If you read that conversation again, you can note where some enthusiasm might be generated. You can see where certain phrases could be said a little faster, and where the pitch of the voice might rise or fall. You might place the pauses in different places, and give some words more attention than others.

The sentences are not long. They bring out emphasis by raising and lowering the voice. Their phrasing is without effort. Communication is complete and understood. But neither person got the point of the sermon! When the subject was changed to John and Debbie, a breath of excitement was on the wire. Everything about the conversation worked.

Conversation works because God made us to be communicators. But sometimes we can't understand each other. The imaginary preacher (above) used words, but there was no communication. Perhaps the sermon was a lecture. The pastor might have depended heavily on notes, distracting the hearers and lacking eye contact to personalize the message.

Perhaps the strongest clue to what was missing was in the comment *"I wish the preacher would just talk to us."* The sermon never got inside of either person. Unlike the fisherman describing his fishing adventure, the preacher was describing nothing—just passing on dry information without opening any gates to the mind.

The fisherman opened gates of imagination, and the hearers drew their own pictures out of the conversation. If the preacher intended to get the mind to move the will, the bridge of imagination was missing. Not only was the bridge out, but the road itself was unmarked. We can see it from the comment *"He rambled."*

Conversation that communicates needs a strong base. Speakers must have enough interest in something so that they want to tell about it. They want to make certain they are understood. The fisherman did, the preacher didn't.

Meaningful conversation allows all the mechanics to work, based on knowing something interesting. It flows out naturally, with qualities that compel hearers to listen.

IT'S LIKE THE LITTLE CHILD WHO SAID, "WE'RE TAUGHT NOT TO RUN IN CLASS—EVEN WHEN THE TEACHER CAN'T SEE US. BECAUSE EVEN IF SHE CAN'T SEE US, JESUS CAN . . . AND HE MIGHT TELL THE PRINCIPAL!"

Let's draw from what is instinctive in all of us, and see if we can apply that creativity to our preaching and teaching.

GOD SET THE CONVERSATIONAL STANDARD

After Moses led the people out of Egypt and before they continued toward the Promised Land, he had some intense conversations with God:

> The Lord used to speak to Moses face to face, as one speaks to a friend. (Exod. 33:11)

Before Moses received the Ten Commandments, he told the people, "The Lord spoke with you face to face at the mountain, out of the fire." Moses told them that he had stood between God and them and spoken God's words to the people (Deut. 5:4-5).

Just as God spoke to Moses in conversation, so also the Bible is a conversation between God and us. Both Testaments report conversations of God through the prophets and the disciples who faithfully recorded what God wanted to reveal about himself and the human condition.

The natural way for God to communicate was through conversation, since he created people with the capability of talking to each other. Paul also says, "God has sent the Spirit of his Son into our hearts" (Gal. 4:6). In Romans 5:5, Paul tells us that through the same Spirit, God has poured his love into our hearts.

Hence, we understand that God wants to be intimate with us and really does talk to us. In fact, the Bible says, "The Lord confides in those who fear him; he makes his covenant known to them" (Ps. 25:14). Now that's real close conversation, isn't it?

Putting all this together, it seems reasonable to recognize that conversation has a place in setting the style by which speakers and teachers approach their listeners.

Let's look at some of the advantages of the conversational approach for communicators.

CONVERSATION CHANGES THE ROUTING

If you send a package by the United States Postal Service for overnight delivery, you can track that package by phone or on the Internet. You can even make a printout of where your package is at any given moment. In the same way, you can track your baggage when you fly. While you're on your way to Dallas, you can see it go to Boston!

The normal routing system for many Christian speakers is a predictable fixed course. The audience knows exactly where the speaker is going. Am I going to beat that system into the ground? Absolutely not! Earlier in this book, I outlined that very idea (chap. 4). But, I warned, as much as an audience is helped by knowing where the preacher is going, such a routing system can become stuffy and rigid.

The conversational approach can change the delivery. It can be accomplished with statements like these:

- Let me tell you a story about . . .
- Do you see what God says here?
- Isn't it interesting that . . .
- Did you know . . . ?
- I am as surprised as you are that . . .
- Maybe you didn't hear me say . . .
- Now here's an idea . . .
- Wait until you hear this . . .
- On the other hand . . .
- Well, it's because . . .

- Can you believe this?
- Maybe you've experienced this also.

The categories of thought are not changed, but you have altered the route by which you get from one marker to the next. You have diced the thoughts with elements of conversation. The closer you get to conversation in your delivery system, the more likely people are to listen.

Why? It's the way people communicate every day!

"Where are you going?" "To the store."
"Did you see the game?" "Yes."
"Did you like it?" "Oh, yeah."
"Honey, I got a raise!" "Wonderful. I'm so glad for you."
"What are you doing this evening?" "Oh, I don't know."
"Well, how about going to the game with me?" "Sure."

Generally, normal communication does not use sentences. It's always to the point. Even when we don't understand each other, the cause is not that we have slipped out of the conversational mode.

Begin listening more carefully to the conversations in your own house. Take note of how you talk to each other. Pay attention to newscasters and speakers on television shows. Then ask yourself, "Is my public speaking coming through as talking or lecturing?"

How about the way you read the Scriptures? Do you read like you talk? Does your reading have the ingredients of pause, rate of delivery, change of tone and pitch, as when you talk? Do you prepare to read with conversation in mind? Be deliberate about this conversational research.

There's another reason why the conversational approach is effective.

Conversation Involves the Audience

If you ask questions of people in the audience, you are more likely to look at them more often. If you read the Bible as though you are talking to the people, you also will be led to look at them.

Hold the Bible up reasonably high. That way you can easily look at the hearers by raising your head slightly for brief eye contact. To keep from losing your place, you can keep a finger on the line you're reading.

Being able to look at the hearers adds a personal touch, assisting your awareness that you are in conversation with them. This will help the audience, and it will help you as well. You will discover you are more relaxed and not as nervous.

When we approach the speaking opportunity by using a talking mode, we are moved to think more about the receiver than the sender. One large telephone company instructed all their operators to smile when they talk with anyone. Psychologists have discovered that the unseen smile can alter even a phone conversation. It changes the attitude. The listeners feel that they are in a conversation, linked to the operator.

Something like that occurs when a speaker moves normal conversational techniques into the structure of a speech. Points one, two, and three should stay in place—the mind responds best to order. But conversation loosens up the insides of the points. The route has been changed.

Being involved with speakers in answering questions or developing thoughts with them is so critical to listening. Minds find it difficult to wander away when they are engaged in a conversation.

Conversation mixes people into the truth being offered. The mind and the bridge of imagination take it to the will, where there is a chance for change. For Christian speakers, conversation beats lecturing every time.

You might even be encouraged by hearing verbal responses such as "Amen, Brother" or "You said it, Sister." In good early-church and Anabaptist tradition, you could invite others in the meeting to weigh, confirm, expand, and test your presentation (1 Cor. 14:29; 1 Thess. 5:20-21). Instead of dozing off, your audience could share in interactive conversation. Such two-way communication would benefit the group and its ministry.

To check yourself for lecturing tendencies, tape your next speaking opportunity. Ask a friend to help you critique your methods. The results will be worth the time and effort.

CONVERSATION OFFERS FRESHNESS

Hearers love the unexpected. The freshness of new approaches to teaching should find their way into every Sunday school class in America. It's time to break out of the stereotypical lesson format and class response. Many sermons could use a dose of life as well.

By simply approaching the sameness with a sprinkle of conversation, the most tired talk can shine with sparkle and brightness when it needs it the most.

In your preparation, think of Aunt Hilda. Imagine that you are going to tell her what you know about God's love. That idea alone will lead you to take a fresh look at the way you prepare.

Like a newscaster, imagine yourself preparing to talk to one person. Pick someone out of your class or congregation and ask yourself, "How would I prepare to talk to that one person?"

It wouldn't look like a lecture, would it? You would try to keep the conversation as simple as possible, and load it with pictured information. Since you wouldn't be so consumed with trying to impress the person, much of the fear and nervousness would disappear.

In conversation you can be intense about the truth without being unfriendly. You are prepared, so you know what you're going to say. Once again, you talk naturally, with no thought of where to add pauses, change voice inflection, or talk faster. It just happens.

Put Aunt Hilda or any specific person into that audience of twenty-five hundred or twenty, and you breathe life into your presentation and individualize it. If you can think "conversation" while you are preparing, you will deliberately add the necessary ingredients such as questions and the unexpected.

For a public presentation, think about the following:

- I just want to talk to people.
- I would like to encourage someone today.
- I want to tell them something.
- I want to help people believe.

Such an exercise will mellow you out. Individuals will be your audience. Harvey doesn't need a lecture; . . . he won't accept it in those clothes, anyhow. If you just talk to him, he'll probably listen and maybe even change.

The entire audience becomes Harvey or Mabel, no matter how many people are included. The speaker sees and talks to someone who is many. When you take this approach, a springtime freshness fills the room. You find yourself thinking about how to deliver the phrases, where to pause, which words need lifting up, and what needs little or no emphasis. If you prepare like that, you will exude a confidence refreshing to your listeners.

CONVERSATION FREES ONE FROM NOTES

My own approach to conversational preaching is to prepare an outline that can be easily memorized. Then I speak to the ideas contained in the structure. I do not write the sermon. It is true that most of the great preachers of days gone by have been manuscript preachers, but that was then. To be conversational in delivery, one needs to be relatively free of notes, I believe.

When I see an announcer advertising a product and a newscaster giving the news, they speak directly to the audience, with eye contact. I recognize that we do not see a monitor and that the speaker often uses a TelePrompTer. Yet we are led to feel that they are speaking directly to us, not reading to us.

For me, the Word of God is so important that I must give my best effort to directness with an audience. As I speak from Scripture, I often have signs in the margin that, through preparation, remind me of an idea.

Likewise, I finally prepare by drawing a circle and placing words that develop the point inside the circle. Then I draw another circle representing the next point and place words inside it that develop that point.

I link however many circles there are with bridge connectors or transitions. In my final preparation, I then visualize the circles and what is inside them so that I basically speak to ideas.

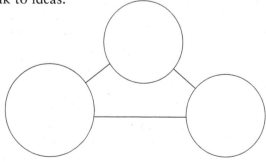

Often I pick up a book and read several lines, or do the same with a magazine in relation to the presentation. If I want to incorporate a statement, I print it, then pick it up and read it. To that extent, I do use notes.

The act of picking up something is in itself a way to hold attention. I show the cover of the book, or the cover of the magazine. If it is a printed quotation, I put it on a full sheet so that it is quite visible.

There are good manuscript preachers, and those who prepare a full manuscript and memorize it for delivery. That is fine as long as such aids are not hiding a fear of failure that might seem to be obvious with those helps.

In class, I always had students preach at least one sermon without notes, just to give them a taste of the freedom. That also helps the students think about whether holding firmly to notes or a manuscript might be connected with low performance and fear of failure.

Speaking without notes *can* lead to meandering. Even worse, it may tempt us to avoid serious preparation, believing that the Holy Spirit will provide. But the Holy Spirit always speaks best through a prepared mind.

Teaching or leading a Bible study naturally requires more use of notes. But conversation is even more natural if something other than a lecture is the format. Questions and answers flow between leader and listeners easily.

With whatever method or in whatever setting, the firm desire to reach listeners always requires leaders to think in terms of the intimacy of talking to people. God has illustrated that throughout the Bible. It is an up-front and personal touch that we must strive to achieve.

In this chapter I have discussed the conversational approach as the most natural choice for speakers. It is a communication tool already in place and at our disposal. Even though we all possess it, most of us have to intentionally introduce it into our public speaking if we are to realize fully its value.

The conclusion is simple: *Get as close as you can to conversation in speaking. It's the surest guarantee of being heard.*

The next chapter is a challenging one. We want to look at how to read an audience. If we learn how to accomplish this, we'll be pleasantly surprised at how confident we can become.

10

ATTENTION

HOW TO READ AN AUDIENCE

L ook out over the audience. Observe all those lovely faces:

- Some are smiling.
- Some are older faces, looking somber and distant.
- Some people hold babies in their arms.
- There are children, sitting next to their parents, trying not to squirm.
- Adults with challenging faces.
- New faces.
- Young faces so innocent, yet so TV-streetwise and probably more.
- Teen faces with an attitude.
- Faces far away in the balcony.
- Angry faces.
- Tear-stained faces.
- Problem-filled stressed-out faces.
- Joyous banquet-table faces.
- Sunday school children's faces.
- An interested face here, an eager one there.
- There's a "show me" face in the back row.

There is a common denominator for speakers in all these settings. We know it from experience. It's called by several names: fear, nervousness, challenge, opportunity.

Why? Fear of failure calls you to march to a different drummer. The beating of the drum tempts you to yield to its call and be scared into not believing in yourself and the Lord (see chap. 2).

The challenge and opportunity to say a good word for Jesus beats a different drum. Its sound offers confidence and self-assurance with only traces of nervousness and fear remaining.

Is it possible to read an audience, marching to that drum of confidence and self-assurance? The answer is yes. That is what this chapter is all about.

In a sentence, here is how to gauge an audience:

READ AN AUDIENCE GENERICALLY, THEN PARTICULARLY.

READING AN AUDIENCE GENERICALLY

Certain facts are true about every person in my audience:

- Everyone will bleed when cut.
- Everyone likes to laugh or smile.
- Teenagers are concerned about life's meaning.
- All of us have religious urgings of some nature.
- People are not necessarily there to hear me.
- Ears and minds are fickle, attracted in many ways.
- Minds cannot concentrate on two things at once.
- People need to sense that we are making progress.
- Listeners may take one idea and discard the rest.

My friend's pet dog is a good example of how an audience can stray, yet not be lost. Stan and I drove down a long country lane from his farmhouse to the main road. As we left the house, his dog Tek followed us. He chased

144 YOU CAN'T HELP BUT LISTEN

after our truck, then disappeared into the woods, probably chasing a rabbit. Soon he reappeared following us again as we drove on down the lane.

Tek was out of sight just before we reached the main road. But when we got there, Tek was waiting for us. Tek knew the track and how to get back to it.

I know there will be people in our audiences like Tek. They will chase a rabbit of an idea from the talk, think about it, and then come back to the talk later. Therefore, listeners need to see that we are on a particular road, and they must want to come back, knowing how to get there.

Here's an important clue:

> **A SNORE IS A GOOD INDICATION
> THAT I HAVE LOST A LISTENER.**

It is a challenge to keep a farmer awake if he got up at four in the morning to milk his cows. Keeping him awake three out of four Sundays a month is a record. But when he does stay awake, it's because he wants to listen and fights sleep. Something worth fighting for is going on inside of him. (By the way, I don't accept blame for sleepers if they're out before I begin to speak.)

I realize many parents bring toys for their children to play with during the service. I also know the adults bring their own mental toys that I can't see. I can never assume that they are not playing with them!

Here are some practical observations about reading an audience in general:

- I try to find out as much about an audience as I can before speaking to them.
- In almost any circumstance, I introduce myself and shake hands with as many people as I can before speaking.

- In a setting over a long period of time, I still greet and shake hands with as many folks as possible.
- Movement of any kind in back of me on the platform or in the audience will take most of the ears and eyes away.
- I bring people back by reviewing a point, without making any indication of what happened, to keep from embarrassing anyone.
- Stories and illustrations hold attention and let in light because they are windows. But with too many illustrations, you'll have no structure or theme. These are "greenhouse sermons," all light and little substance.
- Listening comes from wanting to hear—my preparation must consider that thought.
- If I am going to hold an audience, I must include some elements of entertainment.
- There should be some touches of humor. People need moments of relaxation. The spots must fit.
- Speaking without notes is a more personal approach with a better chance of making people want to hear.
- Television commentators read from monitors. Their intent is to be able to look straight at you, for a more personal touch.
- An object held before the audience for illustration will attract attention.
- An audience looking at me does not guarantee that they are paying attention to what I am saying.
- Any kind of movement I make, spontaneous or otherwise, will attract attention.
- My body will not lie for me. It often tells the audience more than my words.
- If I use names, either of people in the audience or otherwise, ears will listen.
- If I am aware of what is going on in the community,

state, or nation, and filter it into my teaching, my audience will pay attention.

• Even though paying attention is often as difficult as paying taxes, I am sure that using these suggestions will help me.

• The audience pays better attention to me if I pay attention to time. I must quit when finished.

STAND UP! SPEAK OUT! SHUT UP! SIT DOWN!

• I follow the usual time limits. If the audience is used to finishing by noon, I finish at noon.

• When the audience starts reaching for hymnbooks or folding bulletins, I have said something suggesting a near finish.

• I am aware of the importance of closing moments. They have to be deliberate and well planned to avoid early dismissal of the minds.

• If people look at their watches, I may be boring.

• If they shake their watches to see if they are broken, I am in big trouble.

• Audiences have different personalities. Some take humor easily, while others don't. It won't take me long to find out!

• People, no matter how sophisticated, do not like complicated talks because they have to work too hard to understand them.

• I do not take too seriously every compliment I receive after a presentation. Some folks feel compelled to say something. Put all your feedback together and average it out!

• Babies crying will distract an audience. I try to rise above that distraction without embarrassing the parents.

• A Christian audience wants to be captured and held

by relevant material. They need something to help them live more fulfilling lives.

- The message I deliver may not be the one they hear.
- I don't know what I have said until I know what they've heard.
- If there is a choir behind me or a balcony above me, I must look at those people from time to time.
- The children in my audience are precious. They should not be ignored.
- The audience will remember little of what I say.
- People remember images and ideas, not necessarily who said them.
- Large chunks of my audience are biblically illiterate.
- If I announce a Bible passage, I allow time for them to find it before I start to read or speak.
- People will be present who have just been arguing before entering my meeting.
- It takes only three or four people to propel a standing ovation.
- A significant pause can draw people into the talk. If it is long enough, I can even wake up a sleeper.
- Guilt trips can overwhelm an audience, often producing negative results.
- The audience is a mix of Christians, practical atheists, and pagans.
- The audience will include people with disabilities; I must always be sensitive so as to not offend.
- If I prepare with a particular person in mind, that person will not be there.

In these and so many other ways, an audience is generally the same. People need a sense of togetherness. They need the adventure of discovering the Word of God in a body of believers.

READING AN AUDIENCE PARTICULARLY

To get a particular reading of an audience, read yourself. When you pick up a family photo album, where do you usually go first? Usually you will look for a picture of yourself.

You have just read a particular audience. Stated simply, we are all interested in ourselves. That describes your audience from the youngest baby, crying in her mother's arms, to the oldest senior in the room.

All of us go to great lengths to deny it, but what interests us is ourselves. Our attention will be there all the time unless duties are engrossing us. Nothing appeals to me more than me. Unless something more powerful possesses the mind, the drift to daydreams will occur.

Thoughts orbit easily around the ego. The drift takes any turns you allow, centering on a matter of personal concern. Desires, problems, needs, hopes, fears, dreams for success—these are all readily available. No one can escape the lure. No matter what group you address, pick out any face in the audience and know that ego is trying to rule. We all tend to justify ourselves, elevate ourselves, or diminish ourselves. Minds drift to self.

A television show offered money to anyone who could talk into a microphone for one minute without mentioning the words *I*, *me*, *my*, or *mine*. Little money was given away. We like to think of ourselves. I am emphasizing this truth because there is an important lesson we can learn from it:

YOU CAN CAPTURE AND HOLD AN AUDIENCE IF HUMAN-INTEREST STORIES DOT THE LANDSCAPE.

Magazines, newspapers, and television do it all the time. They center on people, what they are doing, where they are going, and how they are living.

Abstract ideas do not appeal to an audience unless they can be understood with the help of people-related comparisons, contrasts, and stories. An audience can be quickly pulled into focus if you name people and mention places and events. Being concrete and particular will make what you say interesting. Generalities will not hold people.

For example, Jesus was specific when he taught:

Everyone then who hears these words of mine and acts on them will be like a wise man who built his house on rock. (Matt. 7:24)

Listeners will consciously or unconsciously ask themselves, "What can that do for me?" If they can see by comparison, contrast, or story how it is of personal value, then their attention is aroused.

Jesus is specific in his use of the house on rock. There is nothing vague about that image.

A particular reading of an audience reveals that everyone is hurting somewhere inside. Like a toothache, it demands attention. No sermon or lesson can touch every hurt. But over time, if the principle of keeping people's interest is kept in mind, then help will be there.

Here's another reason why it's important to know that people are ego-centered:

LISTENERS ARE MORE INTERESTED IN THEIR OWN COUNTRY THAN IN A PLACE THOUSANDS OF MILES AWAY.

Hometown stories are always more attractive than those about a town even a few miles away. There's something about our home street or our own hometown that's magic.

Here's an example from the New Testament. Peter had an experience with a crowd who thought part of their group was drunk. He used the incident to put an old prophecy from Joel into terms that became personal to each one.

By relating the event of Pentecost in Acts 2 to an ancient prophet, Peter was able to show how Jesus fulfills the promised eternal line of David. When Peter confronted the crowd with some responsibility for the crucifixion of Jesus (2:23), they approached Peter and the other apostles. Individually and collectively, they cried out, "What should we do?" (2:37).

Acts says, "They were cut to the heart." What a personal touch! In reality, they were asking, "What does this mean to me?" An old prophecy became new and interesting. Peter made something old look new and personal—thus it became gripping. Both the old and the new can draw attention. In this case, the old prophet Joel was in their town, on their streets, and in their homes. And now, so was Jesus.

All audiences are like that one. They want to know:

- What's in it for me?
- Is what is being offered better than what I have?
- How much will it cost me, personally?
- What will I have to give up?

Here's another reason why it's important to know that people are ego-centered:

INTEREST IS CONTAGIOUS.

If speakers are consumed by what they are saying, the listeners will be infected by the same condition and won't be able to help themselves. When listeners gather for

Sunday school or worship, they do not necessarily bring interest and enthusiasm with them. Thus the speaker has to provide a lot of both!

Sometime when you are a listener, pay attention to the point at which you become interested in the talk. A careful check on this matter will usually show that it was when the speaker was the most interested and enthusiastic.

People will give up their daydreams, but only for a price. It is the speaker's responsibility to give off a sense of knowledge, excitement, and interest. Those are the qualities that command attention within an audience. Here's another reason for ego-centered attention:

PICTURES FEED THEIR MINDS EVERY DAY.

Where there are no pictures, the ego will want something more entertaining, without leaving the room. In hundreds of ads each week, the listeners are being encouraged to become dissatisfied with what they currently possess in favor of something new.

In contrast, arriving for Sunday school class can be quite dull. Unless teachers have prepared themselves to create pictures, the ego will do what it likes to do, feed on itself. That move is so natural, the person will hardly notice it occurring.

When there is sameness, lameness, or tameness in the teacher, the wounds of the listeners will remain intact. Thickness spreads over the group like a heavy fog.

But if you can visualize every person as being interested in the same thing—themselves—then you know how to appeal to everyone.

Let's put all this together. Planning for the meeting or looking out over the audience, I see the people as a group and as individuals. I am not afraid of them. We are two of a kind.

I am going to offer them God's love in its most expressive form: Jesus Christ.

We will both be blessed if we listen. I have prepared. I know what I am going to say. I am confident. I know that "perfect love casts out fear" (1 John 4:18). In the love of God, I love them.

An assurance like that can change your whole perspective on teaching and preaching. It will allow for some spontaneity in your spirit. Your internal impulses will blossom. The Holy Spirit can give you expression when you are that free.

Consider this freedom:

> I proclaim righteousness in the great assembly;
> I do not seal my lips, as you know, O Lord.
> I do not hide your righteousness in my heart;
> I speak of your faithfulness and salvation.
> I do not conceal your love and your truth
> from the great assembly. (Ps. 40:9-10, NIV)

When the writer of Hebrews speaks of Christ in chapter 10, he uses portions of this psalm. For Christian speakers, this passage declares a boldness that all of us ought to claim. What is in the heart is spoken out clearly.

You also can speak confidently to a great assembly. You need to prepare thoroughly, build a simple outline that you can remember, and talk from the ideas that God has given you through the Scriptures.

After preparation, as you talk to an audience with freedom, the element of conversation will be your best tool of communication.

As in conversation, you will be creating as you deliver your ideas. The openness of such creativity allows the Spirit room to be an occupying force, allowing you to be spontaneous and carried along. Nothing can give a speaker more confidence and self-assurance. Nothing!

We have now read an audience generically and particularly.

Reading generically presents challenges that can bring fear, but also opportunity. Knowing general characteristics will always be valuable.

Reading a gathering particularly will give a much deeper level of understanding. All people in all audiences have one basic characteristic that makes them all the same—a tendency toward being centered in ego.

When not challenged, the ego will take over the mind of the listener. Since the mind cannot hold two ideas at the same time, the speaker must compete.

Speakers can gain confidence and freedom by recognizing that this competition exists. Self-assurance comes with awareness that you are talking to a gathering of people just like yourself. Thus you have to be well prepared, talking to them about the one who wants to be in the front-row seat of their minds—Jesus.

The next chapter addresses a subject that speaks even louder than our voice: body language.

11

BODY LANGUAGE

SPEAKING WITH MORE THAN VOICE

Body language is a powerful part of any presentation. Some communication theorists believe it makes up more than 90 percent of our delivery. In any speaking setting, our bodies put on a remarkable display of our inner being by revealing our attitudes, heartfelt beliefs, and emotions. This nonverbal language usually speaks to an audience without effort and mostly without plan. Our bodies do not lie for us. They always tell it like it is.

That truth can keep us honest. We have to match our words with what our body will say for us. If the words don't match our inner being, the body will tell on us. Body language is like a visible conscience for the soul.

CONSCIENCE MAKES YOU TELL YOUR MOTHER BEFORE YOUR SISTER DOES.

To say it another way, believability comes from the heart. Jesus said it this way, "Out of the abundance of the heart the mouth speaks" (Matt. 12:34). We send out signals by our movements, quality of voice, and gestures. These signals suggest honesty and confidence—or they can suggest fear, confusion, and insincerity.

We may think that our words are running the show;

yet our whole body, gestures, and face talk for us and tell the real story. The body has little choice—it has to be honest even if the words flowing from the mouth are dishonest.

Don Knotts, on the *Andy Griffith Show*, was masterful at expressing emotion, attitudes, and feelings. His eyes would open large, like saucers, and you would know he was scared to death. His whole body shouted fear. Without uttering a word, you knew fear was everywhere.

If he was cocky about something, his head would turn, his face would twist, and his mouth would clearly reveal his acting attitude. Thumbs would hook over his belt, and he would draw his body up to full height, showing everyone that he was some dude. No words, just the body talking.

When he acted as a nervous speaker, his entire body quivered and his hands trembled as he held his note cards. Of course, he was acting, deliberately making his body express emotions. For a speaker, body talk speaks for itself, whether we want it to or not. That's why it is our speaking conscience.

Poker players call these body revelations "tells." A book about poker advertised promises to help people identify "tells" such as how to read the hands, changes in the voice, eye contact, and the way the body moves forward suddenly.

Habits are hard to break. Even a little twitch can reveal something about the cards a player holds. Body language is so important to poker players, this book offers more than 170 photos illustrating various tells.

What a Christian communicator has to offer is much more important than how to win at poker. Hence, it is essential for us to think seriously about body language. They are the tells in our nonverbal communication.

The Silent Witness

The body is a silent witness to everything going on inside a speaker. Like a witness in a courtroom, the body gives testimony. Even though your body doesn't have to promise to tell the whole truth before testifying, it is brutally honest. Listeners can view the testimony clearly.

Someone said, "It's not what you eat, but what's eating you"—that's what emerges from a speaker. If you are not fully prepared to speak, you can be sure your body will be a silent witness to that fact. Lack of preparation will eat at you. Confidence will be lacking. Even if you don't shake like Don Knotts, there will be an element of nervousness in your delivery.

Likewise, if there is something you have not clarified when trying to explain a point, your mind will falter, and your silent body will testify against you.

Nevertheless, the silent witness can be used to good advantage for you as well. If you deliberately change your body language, it will change the way you feel. A brisk walk in fresh air can change your feelings; so also a deep breath or a smile can change the way you feel about yourself or your audience.

When the body has experienced refreshment, you feel changed inside. It doesn't take as many muscles to smile as it does to frown! Nonverbal language can even change the way people in your audience feel about you. They will sense your inner strength or weakness. The listeners will discover your body witnessing to your belief system.

The famous Green Bay Packers football coach Vince Lombardi once told his players, "Look good getting off the bus, and then play a heck of a game!" How would a player look good getting off a bus? Probably by walking erect, thinking confidently, acting bold, and seeing oneself as a winner. You can change your insides by making your silent bodily witness talk for you.

Your silent witness will infect your audience. Your interest in your subject is contagious—so also is your body language. The action draws people to you.

It is possible for too much testimony to be given. A teacher can be overactive and disconcerting to the listeners. It's important to avoid annoying movements on one hand, and standing motionless on the other. As a Christian communicator, your silent witness cannot fail you. The testimony will be loud and clear. Your body will say with conviction, "I want to help you believe."

IN YOUR FACE—UP FRONT AND PERSONAL

Isaiah must have had a Clint Eastwood face when he said,

The Lord God helps me; . . .
therefore I have set my face like flint. (Isa. 50:7)

Isaiah's determination was registered in his face. His resolve was an answer to those opposing his prophecies.

People lift and shift and alter their faces to bring back their youth.

THERE'S A NEW ANTI-AGING CREAM:
OIL OF DELAY.

But nothing can keep the face from giving honest testimony in public speaking.

There is a so-called poker face that will not testify about the player's hand. It is a face supposedly without expression. If it can be done, it simply proves the point—you must make a serious effort to keep your face from giving you away.

So, for example, rolling your eyes to the ceiling or to the back wall suggests that you're nervous, or that you can't think while you're looking at your audience. But touching them with your eyes tells the listeners you are genuinely interested in them.

Over time, audiences can get used to minimal eye contact. But it removes a critical element in communication, a closeness so important to speaker and listener. In that case, you may eventually lose your audience.

We can offer Christian truth in well-organized packages that are not delivered because our eyes suggest disinterest or even fear. If you really want to make friends with an audience, then make your eyes obey you.

Obviously, seeing everyone eye-to-eye is not possible, but looking at the audience deliberately suggests a personal touch, whether you are looking at every eye or not. Being intensely interested in your subject will cause your eyes to open wider at times. Eyebrows will rise. The contour of your face will change to match each emotion.

The only plan you need to make it happen is to be clear on your insides about how important the subject is to you. Your face will do the rest—it is the silent witness.

Taking these things into consideration, you must not have a poker face. Either the emotion will break through to the surface, revealing itself through the eyes and face; or a poker face will destroy the impact of the truth to be conveyed. You may be an intensely spiritual person, but being expressionless will weaken your presentation.

As Christian communicators, we must sense how much nonverbal language testifies for us or against us in our teaching.

PUT YOUR HANDS UP

This is not a stickup. Instead, look at how our hands

talk for us, even when we don't say a word. The head makes its own movement with the spoken words, yet hands are the most expressive. They can remain passive or active, based on one's personality.

To be an interesting speaker, you dare not let your hands be passive. If you do, people will sense your lack of urgency, and what you hold to be true will be subdued.

Some people can hardly talk with their hands in their pockets. It's natural for all of us to gesture. If you don't use gestures, some inhibition may have you in a strait-jacket. You may be clinging to your notes or hanging onto the lectern out of fright, making gestures impossible.

The less you use gestures, the more the talk comes off like a lecture. The closer your delivery is to a conversation, the more the body will express itself. The gestures will be as natural as your speaking.

If you hold back your hands when they ought to be saying something, you are likely to become tense. That will be quickly conveyed to your listeners.

Clap your hands and stamp your foot, and say,
Alas for all the vile abominations
  of the house of Israel! (Ezek. 6:11)

Those were the words God used in ordering Ezekiel to speak to the children of Israel. His use of hands and feet helped to capture attention and convey a serious message. They were instruments used to aid the speaker.

Think about all the uses for your hands while you speak. Here are a few to consider:

- Hands can point to things.
- Hands and arms can be extended to shape a cross.
- Hands can measure things.

- Hands can pick up imaginary items.
- Hands can steer a car and shift the gears.
- Hands can be lifted up to God.
- Hands can frame a picture.
- Hands can shake hands with a prophet or disciple.
- Hands can be opened or cradled to suggest God calling or holding us.
- Hands can applaud.
- Hands can be cupped around our mouths to shout.
- Hands can cover our mouths.
- Hands can do invisible magic tricks.

Here's an example of using your hands to illustrate your point. First, explain our inability to see electricity. We can see its effect only in a lighted bulb.

Unwrap an imaginary extension cord and plug it into a socket. Hold up and describe an imaginary lightbulb, including its wattage, just for detail. Then turn on the lightbulb. Like a mime, do everything deliberately.

Turn the bulb on and off several times. Each time tell the audience what you are doing. Ask them if they can see the light. They will answer yes as their imaginations turn it on and off for them.

Explain that we cannot see electricity, only its effect. In the same way, we cannot see God, only the effect in us. Thus, we make the light of God visible.

People will not give their attention to anything else while this illustration is going on. Your hands, without drawing attention to themselves, have illustrated an important point of Christian living.

The use of hands ought to come naturally. As you prepare, think about how to make your hands work for you. The example above was planned in advance. Being total-ly involved in your subject will assure that you won't have to tell your hands what to do. They will testify for you on their own. Yet if you are passive inside, you need not expect your hands to say much.

THE BODY—TURN ME LOOSE

It is interesting to watch people when they are talking. Lips might twitch a little and the nose take an upward turn when some bad-tasting food is described. The eyes might close and the head twist as a friend's unbelievable actions are described. The head of the listener will nod in silent agreement, knowing more of the story.

When you ask such people if they can describe their body motions, they reply, "No, I didn't pay attention to what I was doing!"

Exactly! Those motions all came as natural responses to the words they were saying.

So it is with a public speaker. The body acts naturally, if allowed to do so. Turn the body loose, and it will help you.

To some extent, it takes more than merely turning your body loose. It is a matter of intent, direction, and control. The body should deliver movements that are distinct and make the right impressions at the right time.

For example, you could feel yourself stretching upward, perhaps even rising on your tiptoes, as you express confidence or boldness. The inner sense of self-assurance will bring out some strong body talk.

Teachers are no less compelled to turn their bodies loose to allow full expression. While the circumstances are more intimate in a Bible study gathering or a Sunday school class, the compelling nature of biblical truth pushes the body to give its silent witness.

For example, leaning forward from a sitting position while teaching a Bible study allows the body to convey intensity: "Listen to this! It is crucial!" Before class, the body needs to be unrestrained by fear or lack of confidence. If there is freedom, walking, stamping your feet, kneeling, or any number of positions will suggest themselves. Let yourself do them appropriately.

Being reserved about using your body is one thing—being afraid is another. Your honest confidence that what you are saying is important will make the body react. Only inner restraint will keep you from letting loose.

In any situation, the gestures should be convincing. They should convey what you intend for them. They need to be clear enough to be understood, but not overpowering.

THE SILENT WITNESS—A TOTAL PICTURE

Your total picture is that your genuineness shapes your personal impact. Your sincerity will cause you to be believed or not. You won't be able to define it, and listeners won't be able to say what it is, either. The closest description is that you speak with conviction.

If you could give close attention to what you do naturally, it would be of great value. In normal conversation, how does your body respond to what you are saying? Do your arms move at all? How does excitement move your body while you are talking?

Every time you talk to someone, you are a public speaker. We are always trying to make an emotional impact on a listener, every time we talk.

When an audience is larger than one person, being believed is a matter of how convinced you yourself are of what you are saying. Writing pages of facts may transfer information; to speak effectively to many at once, you must make yourself believable. Indifference, uncertainty, and distrust will build walls against your message.

While describing an accident, what testimony would your body offer? Would your body be passive or active? Would you speak with your arms folded? I doubt it.

Discovering what gestures are normal for you will let you know what you have available in your presentations. Make a video of yourself or ask a friend to critique you.

How do you suppose the gospel spread so quickly after the resurrection of Jesus? Can you imagine for a moment that any of those who saw the risen Lord told the story with their arms hanging at their sides?

Paul tells us that after the resurrection, five hundred people saw Jesus at the same time (1 Cor. 15:6). How animated do you suppose they were whenever they could gather an audience? The whole body was probably invigorated because of the excitement inside. The believability of the witnesses spread the good news.

If you want to impact an audience, people must believe what you say. Obviously, those earliest disciples were believed. Believability is built on emotion. Simply delivering facts wasn't enough to convince people back then, and it still isn't.

Some questions to consider:

- When you are in front of an audience, are you believable?
- Does your nonverbal behavior suggest that you are warm or cold?
- Are you approachable?
- Do you speak love with a clenched fist?
- Do you teach with genuine conviction?
- Do you look grim when you speak?
- Is your teaching just a job? Or do you love it?

The Ultimate Nonverbal Communication

Personal wordless body language is not the entire story. There are other elements that allow you to speak with more than your voice. They are components that surround listeners and also play a part in the involvement of the senses, bringing more complete understanding.

These features are also nonverbal and can be used to good advantage by a speaker or teacher.

The most outrageous and fundamental nonverbal communication is the way God has conclusively revealed his love. Picture Jesus hanging limp and dead on a cross, and then the church (his body) surrounded by the many symbols pointing to that dead-but-now-living Lord.

Within this frame we grasp the highest possible view of God's use of nonverbal language: a crucified and dead Christ and his worshiping body, the church, viewing the silent symbols of the crucifixion and the good news that followed.

Communion exhibits the wonder of the cross most vividly. Those celebrating this victory must be helped to see how the bread and the cup silently point to what they represent. They have meanings without words, and then words are added.

Often without realizing it, speakers and teachers miss the elements that surround a worship service or teaching setting—things that could provide numerous nonverbal foundations to aid them. We are so word-oriented in hymns, texts, prayers, sermons, and lesson plans that we seldom call on the silent symbols to speak.

When we put the expressions of nonverbal worship alongside the words, we provide a greater opportunity for the words to do their work. Words alone have a tough time getting through the crowded highways of listeners' minds.

For example, if a cross is visible to an audience, it probably has become commonplace. Like a piece of furniture in the home, or pictures on the wall, we probably don't notice it anymore. But in your speaking, occasionally bring the cross to life by pointing it out. With the appropriate words and then silence, allow its nonverbal message to give its testimony. The cross unites us with the spectacle of the crucified one. Its wordless testimony, when brought alive by making note of its visibility, can make spoken words powerful.

Stained-glass windows often depict scenes that can be transferred to listeners by allowing them in silence to complete the idea. While these symbols are not body language, speakers can make them deliver their message by pointing them out. In doing so, they can move these scenes from the fringe to the center in our worship.

When an audience stands for the Scripture reading (cf. Neh. 8:5) or to sing or pray, it becomes a nonverbal declaration of worship. The audience will hardly ever recognize it as a deliberate act of worship unless they are reminded of it regularly. Standing offers respect and reverence and demands attention.

Since this posture is so important as an expression without words, the act will be deliberate only if the leader calls for the audience to make it so. For example, say to them, "Let us stand in a deliberate act of worship."

Directing the people to bow their heads in prayer is using another wordless act to draw out reverence before God. Bowing the head is a sign of reverence and submission. Speakers can help the worshipers by identifying the act itself. The leader can regularly offer such a reminder.

Leaders must recognize the importance of this wordless language. Listeners are inclined to depend on words alone unless they are encouraged to do differently.

Point out the Bible that sits on the table near the pulpit. To draw more attention to it, arrange the pictures and furniture differently. Give new meaning to the objects around you. In that way, the audience will be led to appreciate new nonverbal messages in their surroundings.

Consider these items:

- crosses
- windows
- banners
- Bibles
- candles
- incense
- colors
- the communion bread
- the communion cup
- architecture

Allow God's ultimate nonverbal communication, the cross, to be seen, heard, and touched. Make the Scripture visible. Lead your people in understanding why we bow our heads and fold our hands.

We should take nothing for granted in any setting. All the nonverbal expressions of the presence of God need to give their testimony.

In summary, we have seen the implications of the physical body reacting to what the mind is producing through speech. The two must run on the same track. If the heart is close to God, the body will shout "Amen!"

In the next chapter, we see yet another creative way Scripture can come alive before an audience. First-person drama is the subject, but it is not limited to trained actors. It is available to anyone willing to allow personal creativity to be free.

12

DRAMA

CREATIVE DELIVERY

A tall man walked up the aisle where people were gathered for worship. A cane, a limp, a slightly bowed back, and a slow pace indicated age. A broad-brimmed hat, coat buttoned to the top, only a touch of shirt showing, and no tie—these marked a dress code for pastors.

The congregation turned and watched the man proceed slowly to the front of the room, where he turned around to speak. His beard was then more evident; his glasses marked his life era as long ago and far away.

When he introduced himself, he announced that he had tied his horse alongside a hundred other horses and buggies along a rail fence. The nineteenth-century preacher in the broad-brimmed hat took the congregation back in time. He connected their local history with the broader church history, linking both histories to their biblical foundation.

In the same way, you can create your own drama. It will completely change the way you look, speak, and teach. It is an effective communication tool. Creating drama is a project open to anyone with a Bible and a will to change the way Christian truth is delivered to listeners. A drama in the context of a congregation or classroom is not a form to be used week after week, but rather as an interlude. It brings innovation to the regular procedure.

A drama usually has a number of people on a stage, carrying out a sequence of events around a controlling idea. What is developed in this chapter, however, involves only one character, and that very person is the message. The fact that you are the message is the secret to this creative and challenging method of delivery.

The portrayal of a biblical character (see below) is a stimulating and attractive way to bring a person from the pages of Scripture to an audience. They can actually see and hear a lesson from the Bible shaped by how the character is developed. Audiences as congregations or classrooms don't need entertainment to stimulate them as much as they need diversity in the way biblical truth comes to them.

First-person drama is an excellent tool to bring variety into a living-room Bible study, a worship service, or a classroom setting. Each setting is different, but merely in size and surroundings. The person you are portraying is just closer or further away from your people.

Bringing a man or woman out of Bible pages is not all that complicated. You need to have the desire to offer something new and the courage to make it happen.

Changing your appearance is as simple or elaborate as you want it to be. It will take more time in preparation, but since you will be doing such a presentation only occasionally, preparation can be spread out over a longer period of time.

DEFINING DRAMA: FIRST-PERSON TEACHING

The type of drama discussed here revolves around the first person. First person is the speaker who disappears into or becomes "I am" for the audience. The "I" speaks and acts as a character from the Bible or from another period of time meant to portray a biblical lesson.

This is an uncomplicated explanation of a valuable communication tool. It can deliver a Christian message visually, verbally, and emotionally. And one doesn't need more schooling to be an actor!

You can portray any biblical character in the first person. You can depict a character unknown but certainly present during a biblical event. You can dialogue with a Bible character, playing both parts, either by changing positions or by asking questions from a person not seen and then answering them. You can illustrate a point with a brief episode in a presentation, or use drama for the entire speech.

This concept can revolutionize your teaching. You become that "I" as you melt into the biblical or historical character; the audience feels that the person exists.

BIBLICAL CHARACTERS KNOWN AND UNKNOWN

The biblical choices for characters to portray are many. The Bible is all about people and God's desire to make them his own. Obviously, larger-than-life people like Moses or David require an enormous amount of preparation. The good news is that you can choose pieces of the life of either David or Moses, and draw a lesson from the experience. Be realistic in your choices.

Speakers can easily develop Ruth, Hannah, Elizabeth, or Mary from biblical facts. You can even present lesser characters like Cornelius, or Priscilla and Aquila. While there is little information about them, there is enough to create an instructional "I" drama.

You can capture an idea and then decide what person in the Bible might help you develop a story plot. Or you can choose a character and develop a truth from that person. One way is not necessarily better than the other.

Speakers can choose characters to associate with a particular season of the year, or one to make a lesson be a living-person experience. All kinds of people dot the biblical landscape. It's all a matter of choice.

Unknown characters are just as fascinating but more challenging because they have to be created. You could ask, Who tended the sheep while the shepherds went to see the baby Jesus? Did that lone shepherd choose to keep watch, or did the others order him to stay behind? If he volunteered, why did he do so? Didn't he believe? Someone certainly had to stay behind to watch the sheep.

You could imagine how Paul talked to soldiers who had contacts with him. You could use Scriptures to ponder how he might have presented the gospel, given the chance. How would he open the conversation? Would he be bold or shy? Would he ever lament that he missed some opportunities to offer the truth about Jesus?

You could be the girl who accused Peter of being a friend of Jesus on the night of betrayal. Who was she? Did she change after the crucifixion? Was the resurrection a turning point? If she changed, did she tell anyone? What did she say?

Roll your imagination over little-known people of the Bible. You will be surprised at how they will be able to demonstrate an issue or a point for you.

Imagine yourself as a (man or woman) servant in the house of Zacchaeus. Normally we are given a picture of Jesus calling Zacchaeus down from a tree. But as a servant, you can overhear the conversation between Jesus and Zacchaeus. You might explain what made greedy, wealthy Zacchaeus decide to give his money away!

As you can see, there are no limits as to who is available for an "I" to portray. The only limitation is your own imagination. Make a Bible character come alive for your audience. They won't want you to do it all the time, but it's an exciting experience to try now and then.

Open yourself up to "it could have been." Or "it might be." Or "what if?" Release your imagination, and the Bible will speak the truth in an inviting and inspiring manner.

POINT OF VIEW: UNWRAPPING THE PERSON

Once you have chosen an "I" person, the next matter is establishing the character's point of view. How much can you discover about the person from the Bible? A Bible dictionary may be helpful. Would some other materials assist you in your preparation?

If the person is of your own imagination, like the shepherd mentioned above, what is his point of view? What does he think about the angels who appear? What does he believe about the baby that the other shepherds saw? How far do you take him in his belief or unbelief?

There must be a controlling idea around which the character is developed. The shepherd could be made to stay, wonder about the entire event, and be anxious to hear the returning shepherds' story. Or he could disbelieve it entirely.

Once the choice is made of a controlling idea, the next step is to develop the events that bring it to pass. The choice to make the shepherd a believer, unbeliever, or doubter will determine the way you portray the character.

Suppose you choose Hannah for your character. What point of view can you take? First Samuel says as she wept over being childless, Elkanah asked his wife, "Why are you downhearted? Don't I mean more to you then ten sons?" (1:8, NIV). A controlling idea could be the relationship between Hannah and Elkanah. How could having no children affect their marriage?

Another approach might be her decision to present her son to the Lord. What was it like to leave Samuel at the temple, after she had waited so long for him?

When you unwrap a character, you discover as much as you can from the Bible, drawing out what you want the audience to learn. You don't have to have all the answers, or at least not give them. The audience can be left to ponder, drawing their own conclusions.

The shepherd could be a believer, an unbeliever, or a doubter. He could engage in a quest to find out about the baby Jesus.

Hannah could at some point show great frustration with God's inaction. Or you can make her trust shine through her tears.

If doubt becomes the point of view for the shepherd, then it is the controlling purpose. He doubts through all the scenes. Maybe he changes, maybe he doesn't.

Is Hannah joyful or sad when she leaves Samuel with Eli and goes home childless again? Or is she emotionless? Numb? On parting, what does she say to Samuel?

As you unwrap a character, you take whatever cues the Bible offers and build the story around them. As you become that person, you supply the feelings you have chosen for the character. Don't be too quick to think you know how to portray a character.

At this point we have examined the details of the controlling idea and some sense of the sequence of events. Now it's time to talk about what physical and emotional needs are necessary for the character. Allow your mind to talk to your body and voice.

How sad was Hannah? How joyful? How did her body react to her husband when he thought she doubted his love? How sad or joyful was she when Samuel said good-bye? Not just sad or joyful, but *how* sad or *how* joyful? What did her body say?

This makes the preparation real. To become Hannah, you need to get as close as you can to her. Just thinking about her is not enough. Push further.

If Hannah is sad, does her head bow? What about her eyes or her shoulders? What does her voice sound like when she says good-bye to Samuel?

About that guard with Paul, how sympathetic is he to Paul's words about Jesus? Is he telling someone about the experience? What does his voice sound like? Is he animated or listless?

How does the body portray the belief or unbelief of the left-behind shepherd? When the other shepherds come back, is he joyous? If so, what does his voice sound like when he recalls the event?

You need to talk to yourself in advance about these reactions and emotions—it's not all that difficult to do so. The more you go over how a person thinks, how the body reacts, and how the voice expresses itself, the more confident you become about portraying the character.

Unwrapping a person from Scripture means to find details and form a controlling principle. Then go through the full range of emotions, body actions, and voice responses as the story progresses in your development.

You will be surprised at how easily things come together when you want your audience to believe the person exists. What an exciting way to teach biblical truth!

POINT OF VIEW: WRAPPING THE PERSON

Now we are ready to consider several issues.

How Am I Going to Dress?

If the portrayal is a brief interlude within a sermon, simply drape a towel or shawl over your shoulders. Even if the portrayal is the entire lesson, a simple robe of some kind over a suit or dress is adequate. A full costume is certainly appropriate if warranted. The purpose for any change in normal dress is only to aid the audience in grasping the sense of the character, time, and place.

How Am I Going to Enter?

There are many ways to handle your entrance. Someone can introduce you. You can appear, introducing yourself in character at some point. You can enter unnoticed during a prayer. During the sermon or lesson, turn around and add the towel or shawl, announcing who you are.

Would Hannah enter laughing or crying? Would the servant of Zacchaeus enter with a pitcher in hand?

How Am I Going to Stay in Character?

Staying in character has much to do with thinking "I" when you practice. If you are characterizing a Bible or historical person, ponder these questions:

- Am I going to act as if the audience is living in the same time period as I am depicting?
- Shall I refer to places and events they know?
- Am I going to act as if the listeners have no relation to my historical time period?
- If so, are they merely overhearing my conversation?
- Am I alone, simply talking aloud?
- Am I going to act as if my audience will think along with me, like a friend hearing my story?
- Shall I encourage the audience to think of answers to my questions?
- What sort of eye contact should I be establishing with my audience?

- Is my drama my entire message, or just a small portion of my presentation?
- Will I be under a spotlight in a darkened room?

You need to address these sorts of questions in your preparation. In your mind, be clear about what you want for the audience. As you do that, the person you dramatize will become real.

Tell yourself: I really want this person to be a message. I have a truth that this person can develop in a new way. Using drama will help me keep audience attention, so the message has a better chance of being heard. I know I'll be nervous, but the audience will give me energy, and the Holy Spirit will encourage me. I want this presentation to succeed, but even if it doesn't, there's always a next time! I am not putting on a show for applause. My goal is to present truth believably.

Declare your intentions to the Lord, trusting him to help you offer a Bible truth in a novel way.

FIRST-PERSON EXAMPLES

One day while reading Scripture, I decided that the sheep could not care for themselves while the shepherds went to find the baby Jesus. Untended, one sheep might lead the rest astray.

I began with the idea that the sheep were restless because another animal was bothering them or something was about to happen. Then I imagined the shepherds as awestruck with the angels' appearance and message. When they decided to go and find the baby, I became the shepherd left behind because I was skeptical. I wondered who the shepherd was and why he stayed.

In the drama, while the other shepherds are gone, I think aloud about my own beliefs and background, reviewing briefly what I know from the scrolls about God and his people.

When the excited shepherds return, I am only mildly impressed with their message. I am still doubtful. But I gradually change the scene by wondering whatever happened to the baby, noting the number of years that have passed.

Again I change the scene by hearing a preacher who is speaking to large crowds. I reflect on what some people say of the preacher, wondering aloud whether there might be a connection with the baby.

Once again the scene changes as I take a necessary journey to Jerusalem. Arriving there, I note the large crowds for the special days, but I also sense an atmosphere of impending tragedy. I follow the crowd to the crucifixion, still mulling over my doubt. But near the cross there are so many people saying positive things about who Jesus has claimed to be.

I directly refer to all I have seen by recalling the baby. I deliberately turn around, pointing in both directions, from the cross to the baby. I wonder aloud about the two events, allowing the audience time for reflection.

Then I change the scene to the rumors about a resurrection and my uncertainty about such a possibility.

At that point I change the scene once again. I move ahead to groups of people who are meeting on the first day of the week to worship a man called Jesus. I raise the matter of the five hundred who saw Jesus after his death.

In closing, I admit that while I am still doubting, the evidence is strong.

I can present that particular drama in a time frame of from twenty to thirty minutes. I wear sandals, a garment of burlap with a rope around it, and a turban. I carry something vaguely resembling a shepherd's staff.

I try to make people believe I am that shepherd and that while I am skeptical, the evidence is strong. I may just change into a believer.

Another example of drama is one that has particular interest to children. If the children are studying about a certain prophet or Bible character, I can be that person for them.

I have portrayed a prophet being interviewed by children. The prophet was the focus of the lesson. One by one, children would come into the room to ask me questions. They would tell the other children what they had learned from me, many of them returning for follow-up questions. Depending on the ages, sometimes it's better to have the children write out the questions.

My clothing was a modest change—simply a robe and a towel around my head. The change was just enough to recast the atmosphere.

Another first-person drama I often do is a historical enactment of a leader in a denomination over a hundred years ago. Churches celebrating anniversaries of seventy-five or one hundred years often learn a great deal about their congregation.

In preparation, I read as much as I can find about the church leader at that time. Then I attempt to frame the character into myself, as best as I can. My goal is to convince people that I am that leader. It works so well that people begin to wonder about my age!

I dress as close to the historical period as I can. At times I wear a beard, but not always. First-person portrayal is an excellent way to teach history. Since I have studied the congregation's history, I can relate my presentation to its beginnings.

I never try to impress anyone with my acting abilities. My goal is only to make the message believable.

FIRST-PERSON CHALLENGES

The greatest challenge in using drama is your own fear of failing. It is that fear that will even keep you from trying to succeed.

> **I DON'T KNOW THE KEY TO SUCCESS, BUT THE KEY TO FAILURE IS TRYING TO PLEASE EVERYBODY. (BILL COSBY)**

The first person you want to please is yourself. But beware: if you raise your standards too high, you may never accomplish them. Remember that you are not standing alone. If doing a character seems to be what you should be doing in your teaching, then prepare and "just do it." Trust your spirit and God's Spirit.

What will the people think when I appear in costume? No matter what they think, just remember Bill Cosby. Be prepared for some smiles or laughter. If you think it will help, some advance notice of what you will be doing may be appropriate. But surprise has a benefit. You have to be willing to take a chance.

What if I forget what I am supposed to say? These dramas are not so tightly scripted that you have to memorize lines. Plan it in scenes, and remember it in sequence. Think like you are talking to one person about who you are and what you want them to know about your beliefs. Think in terms of ideas, not necessarily lines.

What if people don't like such presentations? How many people are we talking about? Remember Bill Cosby. Consider whether it is wise to clear it in advance with the leadership. How long have you been in leadership there? How free do you feel with them? How adventuresome are you? Are you offering drama too often?

What can I do as a Sunday school teacher? Who is the

subject of the lesson? How much benefit would be gained by a portrayal? Would it be worth the effort?

First-person drama has great potential for almost any Christian gathering. Characters and events abound for the preacher or teacher. They also fit nicely into a setting as small as a living room, with only a few listeners.

It is never a good idea to try to imitate someone else for your own ego benefit. But it is quite effective to become another person when the goal is to teach biblical truth. Delivering a message in this form has great advantage. It is adaptable to the entire lesson or just a portion. You can almost always be sure of attention because you are presenting the material in a fresh way.

You can create or re-create characters known and unknown, from the Bible or from history. The clothing can range from the simple to the elaborate.

Your greatest challenge will be your own fear of failure. Butterflies in the belly are inevitable, but they will slowly fly away if you are willing to try.

> **DO YOU REMEMBER THE TWO FRIGHTENED CATERPILLARS WATCHING THE BUTTERFLY? ONE SAID TO THE OTHER, "YOU'LL NEVER GET ME UP IN ONE OF THOSE!"**

Hopefully, that frightened caterpillar did turn into something that could fly (see the quip in chap. 7). So go for it! Be somebody else.

Now that we've looked at being someone else, it is time to look at being yourself. Who are you before God? That is the most important thing about you. With that truth, we close the book.

13

SELF-EXAMINATION

WHO YOU ARE COUNTS MOST

The key to effective communication is all wrapped up in one important key: being genuine. Check out some of these definitions:

GENUINE: REAL, AUTHENTIC, TRUE, HONEST, PURE, UNADULTERATED, STRAIGHTFORWARD, HEARTFELT, NATURAL, PLAIN, 100 PERCENT.

So, who are you really? Does the real you stand up when it's time for a sermon or presentation? How well do you speak? Here's the key question:

ARE YOU BELIEVABLE? IF YOU AREN'T BELIEVABLE, YOU WON'T BE HEARD.

How can a Christian communicator be anything but believable? Easy. The truth about you will be stronger than the truth you are trying to convey. As the old saying goes, "The truth will out" (cf. Num. 32:23). "Truth will come to light" (Shakespeare, Merchant of Venice).

If your heart solidly agrees with what you are saying, something about you will communicate it to your listeners. So who you are is more important than how well you are speaking. It may even be more important than what you are saying.

Here's a statement on speaking that comes straight out of business communications:

YOU MUST BE BELIEVABLE OR YOU WILL NOT BE HEARD.

For the Christian communicator, here's another way to say the same thing:

YOU MUST BE AUTHENTIC OR GOD'S TRUTH WILL BE LOCKED OUT.

There used to be a saying about a good salesman: "He could sell straw hats to Eskimos." That is an exaggeration, as well as being politically incorrect, but it does represent some elements of being believed. It even suggests persuasiveness without honesty.

But in the context of Scripture, that's not enough. The Bible is what God said, and the gospel is what God said in Jesus Christ! We don't need dishonest persuasion—we need authentic believability. We are more than straw-hat salesmen.

Think of it this way: It's not so much what you do, but how you are with an audience. Who are you before your listeners?

The psalmist declared himself:

My heart is steadfast, O God,
    my heart is steadfast. (Ps. 57:7)

That sort of heart flow accompanied by an impassioned delivery will move a speaker from "can't be listened to" into the category of "you have to listen" because the speaker is so compelling.

Everyone wants to be a good communicator. But remember (in chap. 1) our three groups of speakers?

1. Those you can listen to, with difficulty.
2. Those you can't listen to at all.
3. Those you can't help but listen to because they are so genuine.

To get to that third classification, you absolutely have to be totally convinced about what you are saying. There must be strong evidence of conviction, even if you are by nature a calm and gentle person.

Let's look at five examples from the Bible that represent what it takes to be believed.

AUTHENTICITY SHOWN IN SCRIPTURES

• Read the words of the psalmist, speaking so passionately from his heart:

Hear this, all you peoples,
    give ear, all inhabitants of the world,
both low and high,
    rich and poor together.
My mouth shall speak wisdom;
    the meditation of my heart shall be understanding.
                                    (Ps. 49:1-2)

• In the second example, observe a woman of great power and integrity. Her name was Deborah. She was a prophetess, literally an inspired woman. She bravely led Israel out of despair. Trusting in God for deliverance from the enemy, she led an army, carrying out God's will. Read her story of inspiration in Judges 4 and 5.

• The third example reveals a woman of great spiritual strength, a true servant of God. Mary, mother of our Lord, is a woman of incredible spiritual power. She said,

> My soul magnifies the Lord,
>   and my spirit rejoices in God my Savior
> for he has looked with favor
>   on the lowliness of his servant. (Luke 1:46-48)

• The fourth example is the Lord Jesus himself. As a communicator, he was without peer. His hearers sensed his authority. The people were amazed at his teaching, because he taught them "as one having authority, and not as the scribes" (Mark 1:22).

• Fifth, the apostle Paul also speaks with conviction:

> I was appointed a herald. . . .
> I suffer . . . for this gospel.
> I am not ashamed. . . .
> I know the one in whom I have put my trust. . . .
> I am sure. . . . (2 Tim. 1:11-12)

> We try to persuade others. . . .
> The love of Christ urges us on. (2 Cor. 5:11, 14)

> I am a better [minister] . . .,
> with . . . far more imprisonments,
> with countless floggings, and
> often near death. (2 Cor. 11:23-29)

What these people all have in common is their absolute desire to be in public what they are in private—close to God. That desire burned through their speaking.

Everything about the person revealed that inner resolve.

While these are outstanding examples of dedication, we dare not let them discourage us from attaining our own level of determination. We must be committed to the truth about God in Christ Jesus.

Intensity and earnestness for a preacher or teacher is like the difference between a low flame burning and a house on fire. There is an urgency felt by the audience that is apparent.

Why is it that who you are is more important than how well you speak? It is because people responsible for transmitting God's truth must have internal matters settled about what they really believe, or God's truth will be shut out. You have to be believed to be heard.

Why is it that Christianity, revolutionary and radical by nature, could come to the place called church that people pass by on Sunday? They laugh at you if you tell them there is a revolution going on and that the radical gospel is changing people in that house of worship.

Something has become unbelievable. Mr. and Mrs. General Public sense a lethargy and lack of conviction in today's church. The results of the revolution are not apparent on the street.

Those of us who lead people to think about God must inquire into our own being to make certain of our own persuasion about God and his revelation.

This book is designed to carry you through paths that will make you a better speaker and teacher. These words are my attempt to enable you to understand how important your own person is to the message your voice and body are delivering.

A LOOK AT WHERE WE'VE BEEN

Looking back in review, chapter 1 exposed the need to hold the Scripture as truth. Getting truth is difficult these days, because the modern world assumes that truth is of our own making: "Your truth is yours, my truth is mine." This is a natural result of losing our reference point, the Bible. We have lost what God has said and have ended up in separated positions.

In fact, the man of the Bible, Jesus Christ, is himself truth, as he says, "I am the way, and the truth, and the life" (John 14:6). That truth of Scripture is not readily accepted anymore. Sadly, many who preach or teach are not convinced of the Bible's relevance or its author.

If you can't help but listen to certain speakers or teachers, it is because they are compelling persons. Their preparation is evident, and their desire to communicate is obvious.

> **SPEAKERS ARE COMPELLING WHEN THEIR PREPARATION IS EVIDENT AND THEIR DESIRE TO COMMUNICATE IS OBVIOUS.**

Listening comes from wanting to hear. A speaker has to "buy" the ears and minds from any number of competing influences in the minds of the listeners. You need to win the privilege of being heard.

Scripture in your hands in front of an audience is an awesome responsibility. When you recognize that you have the Bible and grasp the story of everlasting salvation, that produces an energy in you that is evident.

In chapter 2 we looked at fear of speaking. It is a serious enemy, keeping many from taking part in the joys of public presentations. Fear always reduces anyone to a position of weakness. The more fear, the more weakness. Some nervousness is always present and not necessarily bad, unless it becomes overpowering.

One of the surest ways to control your fear is to be

well prepared. With a good grasp of the biblical truth and a desire to help people believe, you become credible. The confidence emerging will astound you. With that assurance, the audience itself will energize you, sensing your integrity.

The big bear of fear is the fear of failure. Again, preparation will tame that bear. If God is your witness, then his Spirit will support you mightily.

In chapters 3-5, the emphasis is on the significance of preparation. With the Scriptures as a starting point, and structure as the base from which to speak, imagination can put color into the images so the listeners can "see" the Scripture.

The Bible is always the place to begin when you want to help people. It's not merely a reference, but a starting point. We should delight in what the Creator has to say about his provisions for us. Digging out the details produces a gold mine of information. Putting those details into an orderly and easily remembered structure sets you going on the road to confidence.

It helps if you remember that every category heading is a promise you make to your listeners. Thus, everything in that category must belong there.

If you allow your imagination to draw pictures from the Scripture, your audience will be able to say, "Now I see what you mean!" The mind is a picture gallery—the listener will either be drawn to what you are painting or be looking at their own drawings.

By all means write out a summary power statement. It should be one that gathers all the thoughts into a sentence of about fifteen words. Funneling all the thoughts into one statement will produce an enormous amount of self-confidence.

More tools for preparation are included in chapters 6

and 7. Visuals and humor are excellent vehicles to use in gaining and holding attention.

Any setting is a natural place for the use of a visual. The Bible offers so much appeal to the eyes. It's a shame that we don't make more use of objects by which to teach. Bible study groups, sermons, and lesson plans can be enhanced with an object people can see. We are all just like children. Objects attract us.

Humor is a loosening tool. It opens minds for serious things, lightens the load, and gives breathing space.

> **WHY DID THE LITTLE GIRL EAT BULLETS?**
> **BECAUSE SHE WANTED TO GROW BANGS.**

You can learn humor if you read funny items anywhere you find them. Look for the funny side of life. Remember that humor has two faces: what you see and what else you can see in the situation.

Don't force humor by trying to be funny. Cultivate what makes you yourself laugh or smile.

Chapters 8–12 develop the importance of a speaker's integrity, the value of a conversational approach in delivery, how audiences respond, allowing the body to act naturally in speaking, and the merits of first-person drama.

As a Christian handling the Bible before an audience, you need to be yourself, with your integrity built upon God's truth and the Holy Spirit's leadership.

The closer you can come to conversation in your public speaking, the more certain you can be of being heard. You can't do this by following a rigid outline without adding some spice. It's a mistake to think you can just "tell people the facts." That won't change them.

If people are listening to a speaker, it is because they want to listen. So the more natural you deliver your words, the more likely you are to be heard. It's that simple.

Sometimes your body will say more than your mouth. Every idea put forth is accompanied by communication from your eyes, your lips, or your nervous smile. Your hands and arms offer their own version of what you are saying, and so does your posture.

Your body should speak with you. If you are being natural before your audience, your body will conform nicely.

First-person drama is not something you would do regularly because of the preparation time and risk of saturating the audience. But occasionally you can pick out a Bible character and create a story form that illustrates what the Scripture is saying.

Two of your greatest enemies are worrying about what people will think and the fear of failure. Preparation, imagination, and a will to do it will be your greatest friends.

> **YOU WOULDN'T WORRY SO MUCH ABOUT WHAT PEOPLE THINK OF YOU IF YOU KNEW HOW SELDOM THEY THINK OF YOU.**

CONCLUDING THOUGHTS

It's a satisfying feeling to be in the category where people can't help but listen to you. Helping you develop and hold onto that feeling is the entire panorama of God's footsteps through biblical history. It all leads up to Jesus, and then he walks with us into eternity. The very thought of it makes the handling of God's Word an exciting adventure.

Think of that small band of chosen people known as the Jews. They were living relatively unknown by the rest of the world; they were set apart and then became a nation led by God. Eventually their people produced the Jew named Jesus. He changed the world so that even atheists have to date history B.C. and A.D.

"How odd of God to choose the Jews" (anon.). How odd, indeed! Even God admits it is odd.

> Ask now about former ages, long before your own, ever since the day that God created human beings on the earth; ask from one end of heaven to the other: has anything so great as this ever happened or has its like ever been heard of? Has any people ever heard the voice of a god speaking out of a fire, as you have heard, and lived? Or has any god ever attempted to go and take a nation for himself from the midst of another nation, by trials, by signs and wonders, by war, by a mighty hand and an outstretched arm, and by terrifying displays of power, as the Lord your God did for you in Egypt before your very eyes?
>
> To you it was shown so that you would acknowledge that the Lord is God; there is no other besides him. From heaven he made you hear his voice to discipline you. On earth he showed you his great fire, while you heard his words coming out of the fire. And because he loved your ancestors, he chose their descendants after them. He brought you out of Egypt with his own presence, by his great power.
>
> (Deut. 4:32-37)

Can we capture that expanse of our heritage through Israel? And through the specific line of David to Jesus? And to the church, his body? And on until, like Enoch, we are walking with God and join that great "cloud of witnesses"? (Gen. 5:24; Heb. 12:1).

If we can view the magnitude of that historically connected series of events, it will make a difference between passion and fire. Passion like happiness can be momentary. But fire is like joy. It stays, not dependent on circumstances. Perhaps that's what Nehemiah had in mind by saying, "The joy of the Lord is your strength" (Neh. 8:10b).

Being with God, the written Word, the living Christ, and the Holy Spirit will bring joy and fire. No one who speaks God's truth can put his story together in written or visible form and remain merely a smoldering ember.

To catch fire is to be—

• overwhelmed
• overcome

To be in awe because—

• God said this
• God did that
• God is doing this now
• God is going to do this in the future
• God knows my name
• God wants to use what he has given me

Spontaneous combustion can start a fire, but circumstances have to be just right. So it is with a speaker. We need to be prayer-soaked, mind-prepared, heart-yielded human beings. If so, we can calmly or excitedly present the Word, and the audience will know that we are on fire.

A burning bush was a history lesson for Moses. God said, "I am the God of your father, the God of Abraham, the God of Isaac, and the God of Jacob" (Exod. 3:6).

Moses was so overcome by the God of his ancestors that he hid his face, afraid to look. But Moses was not satisfied with the voice nor the burning bush. He wanted more of God.

Even the experience on Mount Sinai, receiving the Ten Commandments, was not enough. God also knew Moses' name and was pleased with him, but that still wasn't enough.

So intent was Moses on having more of an inner sense of the presence of God that he made one final plea: "Show me your glory" (Exod. 33:12-18).

All of us who are passing on the words of God have a responsibility. We must be privately what we are publicly. It's the "who" of what is being said. In private we develop that quality known as believability. That is what we reveal in our speaking. As Jesus said, "What comes out of the mouth proceeds from the heart" (Matt. 15:18).

Genuineness is a heart matter. Who you are is more important than how well you speak. Let the word of God discern and shape the intentions of your heart (Heb. 4:12-13).

So who are you, really?

**SEEK TO KNOW THE LORD
AND PRACTICE WHAT YOU KNOW.
THEN YOU WILL BE IN PUBLIC
WHAT YOU ARE WHEN ALONE.**

FIFTEEN COMMANDMENTS FOR PREACHING

GRACIA GRINDAL

(The following are tips on preaching gathered from a variety of people around the church who have some sense of what does and does not work in sermons.)

1. **Did Jesus need to suffer and die for this sermon to be preached?** If not, don't waste your time—or ours—with it. It's probably just clean mental health for religious people.

2. **Never speak of yourself in the tub, shower, or in bed.** It's hard enough for parishioners to follow a sermon without imagining the preacher in the altogether.

3. **Never start your sermon with "When I was asked to preach. . . ."** Drawing attention to your effort preparing the sermon will create too much interest in whether or not it was worth your time—or theirs.

4. **Never start a sermon with an "I."** It's God's Word you're proclaiming, not your own. A way to check how you're doing is to count the number of times you say "I." Remember, there is someone sitting out there doing just that.

5. **Never say, "It's hard to find any gospel in this text."** It will make you seem like an athlete of the text if you happened to find some, giving the impression that you are going to do something really hard, for which you, not God, should be praised. God wasn't clear, is the implication, although you are.

6. **Never begin, "Her name was Jill" or "The water rippled brightly as we stepped into the lake."** It's the homiletical equivalent of "It was a dark and stormy night." If you can tell stories well enough to keep a congregation interested for ten minutes, you're in the wrong business.

7. **Never tell a bathroom or bedroom joke in the pulpit,** especially on Ash Wednesday or Maundy Thursday. It is always inappropriate, but on these days it really wrecks concentration.

8. **Never preach on love after you have had an argument with your congregation, or even one person in it.** Even if you think you were in the right, it sounds like special pleading and usually burdens the conscience of your opponent. Any group will have its disagreements. Disagreements are not sins that you have been given the keys to bind and release. Most sermons on love turn out to have the subtext "You haven't been very nice to me." Your work is to relieve the burdened conscience with the forgiveness of sins. Burdening the consciences of your people so you can come out in the right is an abuse of your office.

9. **Never start a sermon with "And now we begin our Lenten journey."** The gospel is not a mood piece set into the more important liturgical year. You are preaching the Word, not the season.

10. **Never preach an Easter sermon dressed up like an Easter bunny,** or use any secular holiday trimmings for a high holy day. A long time ago, Christians thought these symbols were pagan, or at least inappropriate for church.

11. **Remember the bon mot: "Other people's love is disgusting."** You may think you are the most interesting person in the world, but how interesting you are to others tends to diminish, usually, the further away you are from their bloodline, unless you are a movie star or a royal.

12. **Always assume someone is listening to you for dear life.** They may be dying, or helping someone who is. Don't assume all the hurting people have stayed home and those sitting before you have come to be told they need to do more for others. They may, in fact, have come to be strengthened for the work they are already doing and don't know how they can manage.

13. **Always remember no one hears a thing you say after the noon whistle blows.**

14. **Always assume that someone out there is counting to one hundred [and doing that] five times to make the time pass more quickly.**

15. **Always mention the name of Jesus at least once.** Assume when you preach that there is a life-and-death struggle going on in the heart of someone in your audience who needs Jesus Christ.

(From *Word & World: Theology for Christian Ministry* 19/1 [Winter 1999]: 73-74. Used by permission.)

RESOURCES

FOR PREACHING, TEACHING, AND WORSHIP MINISTRIES

Blamires, Harry. *The Christian Mind: How Should a Christian Think?* Ann Arbor, Mich.: Servant Pubns., 1997 ed. with study guide.

Craddock, Fred B. *Preaching.* Nashville: Abingdon, 1985.

Dockrew, Karen. *Youth Workers Guide to Creative Bible Study.* Rev., exp. Nashville: Broadman & Holman, 1999.

Ezell, Rick. *Hitting a Moving Target.* Grand Rapids: Kregel Pubns., 1999.

Grindal, Gracia. "Fifteen Commandments for Preaching." *Word & World* 19/1 (Winter 1999): 71-82.

Hogan, Lucy Lind, and Robert Reid. *Connecting with the Congregation: Rhetoric and the Art of Preaching.* Nashville: Abingdon, 1999.

Malphurs, Aubrey. *Doing Church: A Biblical Guide for Leading Ministries Through Change.* Grand Rapids, Mich.: Kregel Pubns., 1999.

Moehlenpah, Arlo and Jane. *Teaching with Variety.* Hazelwood, Mo.: Word Aflame Pr., 1990.

O'Day, Gail R., and Thomas G. Long. *Listen to the Word: Studies in Honor of Fred B. Craddock.* Nashville: Abingdon, 1998.

O'Day, Rey, and Edward A. Powers. *Theatre of the Spirit: A Worship Handbook.* New York: Pilgrim Pr., 1980.

Powers, Bruce P., ed. *Christian Education Handbook.* Rev., updated. Nashville: Broadman & Holman, 1996.

Shaw, Susan M. *Storytelling in Religious Education.*

Birmingham: Religious Education Pr., 1999.

Shenk, David W., and Linford Stutzman, eds. *Practicing Truth: Confident Witness in Our Pluralistic World.* Scottdale, Pa.: Herald Pr., 1999.

Thomas, Steve. *Your Church Can Be . . . Family Friendly: How You Can Launch a Successful Family Ministry in Your Congregation.* Joplin, Mo.: College Press Pub. Co., 1996.

Wiersbe, Warren W. *Classic Sermons on Stewardship.* Grand Rapids: Kregel Pubns., 1999.

Wogaman, J. Philip. *Speaking Truth in Love: Prophetic Preaching to a Broken World.* Louisville: Westminster John Knox, 1999.

Zuck, Roy B. *Spirit-filled Teaching: The Power of the Holy Spirit in Your Ministry.* Ed., Charles R. Swindoll. Dallas: Thomas Nelson, Word Pub., 1998.

_____. *Teaching as Paul Taught.* Grand Rapids: Baker Bks., 1998.

THE AUTHOR

Since age twenty-four, Charles R. Munson has been involved in preparing and delivering public talks and sermons. As National Youth Director for the Brethren Church, he spoke to youth rallies and youth groups in local congregations and national gatherings.

For thirty-five years, Munson was a professor at Ashland (Ohio) Theological Seminary, teaching future preachers and teachers how to present God's Word with imagination and conviction.

Pastorates, Bible conferences, banquets, Bible studies in homes and camps—these all provided challenges for Munson to develop skill in packaging words that would create listening ears and minds. He has also published articles in church periodicals. Munson was born in Winber (Johnstown), Pennsylvania, where he lived until moving to Ashland to pursue education for Christian ministry. That ministry has included teaching at Ashland, pastorates, serving as District and National Moderator for the Brethren Church, and as President of the National Association of Brethren Elders, and participating widely in local, district, and national boards and offices.

His education includes college and seminary degrees from Ashland University and Seminary, a master's degree from Pittsburgh Seminary, and a Ph.D. from Case Western Reserve University in Cleveland.

After retiring from Ashland Seminary, Munson has served six Brethren congregations as an interim pastor. Following his wife's death, he moved to Goshen, Indiana, where he pastors a local Brethren congregation.